C³ Creating Conscious Connections

Dr. Cyrina Bullard

Catch Happiness
Publishing House

C³ Creating Conscious Connections

Second Edition

Published by Catch Happiness Publishing House

Copyright © 2020 by Dr. Cyrina Bullard.

ISBN: 978-1-7343693-7-3

Cover art by Tucker Eason -TuckerEason.com

Cover Layout by Dan Katai - Kataicreative.com

Author Photos by Garrett Hacking - PhotographyG.com

QUANTITY PURCHASES: Schools, companies, professional groups, clubs, and other organizations may qualify for special terms when ordering quantities of this title. For information please email Cyrina@CatchHappiness.com

This book is printed in the United States of America

Dedication

To my reader, may you

Create Conscious Connections and

Catch Happiness on your journey.

Acknowledgments

I have a vast amount of gratitude for all the help, encouragement and guidance I have received on my journey! I feel tremendous amounts of appreciation for my sister, Malena, her knowledge, dedication, time, immense efforts, and LOVE! My Mom, Jason, Justin, Tim, Rob, and Neide are also big players on my gratitude list! All my friends were incredibly supportive and instrumental in my healing! Extremely thankful to Mark in Vail who stopped and saved my life! I would also like to thank the family and friends who wrote excerpts for the book: Margie Bullard (Mom), Malena Bullard (sister), Diane Collinet (friend) and Shawna Birdsall (family and friend).

Thank you to Diane, Liz, and Kerry for your immense help and guidance with the edits of this book, I truly am so grateful to each of you for your knowledge and assistance! And deep thanks to my friend, Natela, for being so supportive and helpful during this project! Her technology skills and tutorials were a gift, I have such gratitude! Thanks to James for advancing me in the world of Microsoft® Word! And, finally, to the many friends who read through chapters of the book and gave feedback and guidance I am so grateful: Natela, Nicole, Geordie, Jim, JV, Linda, Gary, Rob, Kathy, Mary, Helen, and Renee for their help and direction! I also want to give a big shout out for all of the people who have helped me on this journey. (You know who you are). Your generosity and help are greatly appreciated!

Medical Disclaimer

The author and publisher have made every effort to ensure that the information in this book was correct at press time. Although, in the world of science information tends to shift and change. The author and publisher do not assume and hereby disclaim any liability to any party for any loss, damage, or disruption caused by errors or omissions, whether such errors or omissions result from negligence, accident, or any other cause. This book is not intended as a substitute for the medical advice of health care providers. The reader should regularly consult their medical provider in matters relating to his/her health and particularly with respect to any symptoms that may require medical attention.

This book contains the opinions and ideas of its author and the people referenced. It is intended to share helpful and informative information on the topics addressed in this book. It is sold with the understanding that the author and publisher are not engaged in rendering medical or health services in the book. The reader should consult his or her medical, health, psychologist or other competent professional before adopting any of the suggestions in this book or drawing inferences from it. The author and publisher specifically disclaim all responsibility for any liability, loss, or risk, personal or otherwise, that is incurred as a consequence, directly or indirectly, of the use and or application of any of the contents of this book.

Preface

Connection with ourselves, others and our world, is a huge influencer in our lives and an element to help create happiness. The cover of this book is an illustration of this with many layers and meaning which started with a connection. In March of 2019, while cruising along at 30,000 feet in the air, I met a nice guy, while flying from San Diego to Denver. We had a very intriguing conversation and experienced a connection. Before we landed, he asked me out on a date. Ever open to possibilities, I said yes. The following weekend he drove four hours to come to Denver. We went on a date and I was excited to see what would evolve. We had very real, open and great conversations; however, unfortunately, that (ever so important) element of chemistry was missing. No chemistry.... although there was a connection. Our serendipitous time together had layers, through one conversation, another connection was created. While together, he shared his relative Tucker Eason's artwork with me. I was impressed and drawn to his work! Tucker, only 29 years young, is an amazing artist and an old soul. One thing led to another and now he is the artist that created my book cover. You never know where connections will lead or why people are placed on your path. This inspires me to encourage us all to be present and open to the possibilities.

The meaning behind the painting *"Edison,"* and the cover of my book, has many elements. The circuits are to illustrate connections. Whether it is a connection with nature, ourselves, our friends or others, there is energy created. There are three circuits, which can be extrapolated to many things: The mind, body and spirit, the Holy Trinity, me almost dying three times, or even the personal, professional and spiritual elements in life. These circuits can equal whatever meaning you would like to associate with the creation of energy in your life. There is a compass at the top of the light bulb to illustrate the question, what path will you take? Below the light bulb is the world globe to allow us to question, where will our path lead? The light bulb has detailed filaments to illustrate a conductive wire to exemplify my two brain injuries and the neuroplasticity and rewiring of the brain! There is a reflection of a window in the lightbulb to illustrate looking out on your life. The overall visual is darkness going to lightness and encouraging us all to follow the path that leads to lightness.

The creation of connections with nature has been a huge player in my life and has led to many different outcomes: once-in-a-lifetime adventures, beautiful inspiring surroundings, and getting three new starts in life. There was a day when the sky opened up and I was struck by lightning and there are two other occasions when I became very connected with nature and almost died. Through this book, I will take you on a journey of my three, close to death experiences. Attention will be focused on the incredible lessons I have learned on my path to hopefully help, comfort, inspire and encourage others.

May this book give us all gratitude for our lives and expansion in our hearts. Let us allow ourselves to be the best we can be and share our gifts with the world. Granting each of us the ability to create magical moments!

Contents

Chapter 1

Let's Begin…

Life's journey is an interesting blend of ups and downs, as well as a series of recollections, reflections, and revelations. Every moment you spend living is a gift and this life is worth the pain when it is intertwined with all the joy, love, excitement and happiness that comes your way. Don't forget to check in with yourself from time to time and make sure you are allowing yourself to live in the moment with gratitude as well as engagement and growth. Experiencing these states of mind and sharing them with the world around you will allow for more positive energy to be generated and oneness.

Going through challenging times allows us to learn fresh lessons, shift attitudes, and new opportunities often appear. Life can seem very daunting, especially during painful times. However, with the right mindset, grit and the correct tools, we can deal with challenges successfully and expansion will occur. The light will eventually shine!

I have almost died three times. That's right, three times! Yet, here I am! My approach to life has changed and I now actively try to live life to the fullest! The fact that I am still here despite facing extreme challenges, has made me quite introspective. Being forced to reassess my purpose in life and to continue to search for the answer to the age-old question: "Why am I here?"

Through introspection, expressing my story to you, and imparting the incredible lessons that I have learned along the way, is a calling. My hope is that in some way my story will resonate within you and bring light and more happiness to your life.

Often, life seems akin to looking at a beautiful garden from a distance. All you see is the beauty and the flowers in bloom, everything appears to be spectacular. It is only upon closer inspection that you realize there are always spots left unattended. The garden has zones that are dry and areas dominated by wild shrubbery and weed overgrowth. These areas cry out to be nurtured. The weeds are analogous to fear. The weeds at times can strangle the growth of the beautiful flowers, just as fear can strangle our dreams and not allow them to flourish.

As you continue your walk in the garden, you see many flowers; each is as beautiful as the previous one. However, not all flowers come without peril. Some flowers have thorns, the same way that life is a mixture of pleasant moments followed by painful ones. This serves as a reminder that life is not always a flower in full bloom; there are obstacles along the way that must be overcome. These obstacles can cause us to either expand with growth or contract. Many times, when we look at someone else's life from a distance, it appears ideal. However, the reality may be quite different from our perceptions. This is because we all have parts of our lives that we have neglected and they need to be nurtured. At times in our own garden of life, we do not allow ourselves to come into full bloom because of fear of the unknown.

My journey has been no different. It is a collection of unexpected obstacles, remarkable lessons, and glorious moments spent in the company of incredible people (and some not-so-incredible ones as well). Many times, when beautiful roses arrive, we are surprised when we are pricked by the thorns. The thorns are part of these exquisite flowers which can be a prompt to remind us that there are two sides to life. What side will you focus on?

We all have our own unique layered beauty. When one is being closed off by either a lack of openness, vulnerability, confidence, transparency or honesty, this can diminish or discolor the layers of our beauty. Many people tend to be emotionally closed off because of painful past experiences that have pricked them one too many times. However, if you can accept that this is your life and that you are in charge, then you can ignite your expansion. *How do you want to spend this journey?* Being true to ourselves and those around us, regardless of a painful past, will help our garden of life flourish. Know that you are NOT your past; we all can create a fabulous future! I'm an extremist; my 'extreme' tendency is that I am ridiculously open and, at times, a little too honest. Occasionally, I even scare people away because of my frankness and willingness to speak about almost anything. In fact, I draw people into conversations that might be, at times, bordering on inappropriate. I now preface certain conversations by saying, "Hey, please set a boundary for me, if you are not comfortable with this topic."

Adopting this approach of granting boundaries to be set, hopefully, allows everyone to feel comfortable. People are truly very interesting. How they think and why they think as they do, fascinates me. There are times I may not agree with someone's thoughts or opinions, although always trying to be respectful. I strive to gain an understanding of their views and be accepting of the human behind these views. On multiple occasions, people have told me that they have never opened up to someone so quickly. After hearing this, I feel honored, as well as compassion for them. I imagine what people have shared with me are the concerns, obligations, and anxieties that they have been carrying around in their hearts for far too long. These are emotions that can trap you and they need to be unburdened for you to feel free.

At times, we may not be in control of the things that occur in our life, although we have control over how we respond to the situation at hand. Science says that the philosophy of "being in the moment" can truly help our overall level of happiness. If there is one thing that my journey has taught me, it is the importance of allowing myself to be present for this life.

In life, we experience and discover many lessons along the way. How can we let our experiences expand us, rather than being in a state of contraction? Our short lives need to be embraced and celebrated. We can do that by being the best that we can be while we are living this gift of life that we have been granted. If we are not living in the moment, we are most likely missing out on innumerable magical gifts.

This book is my story. It will share the amazing path I have traveled and the lessons that I've learned along the way. I have profound gratitude for the multiple rebirths that have been granted to me in this beautiful, unpredictable, challenging, yet amazingly rewarding journey. By living life in the present and with gratitude, I have found happiness.

Different perspectives emerge when each of us looks at and assesses a specific situation or part of our life. How do you evaluate a situation you have to deal with? Do you use a contracted or an expansive lens? Are you kind to yourself and others during the process?

It costs us nothing to be nice to a stranger, or give a sincere compliment to a person when we are going about our daily errands. Questions to ask ourselves: *Have I held the door open for someone and smiled at them today? Did I tell a joke to bring laughter to others? Have I helped myself or someone else to recognize his or her self-worth? Do I volunteer for a cause that I feel is important?*. These are small acts that are expansive, with the potential to facilitate a win-win scenario in life. We never know what good these acts might bring our way, nor the positive impact these kind acts will have. Through the ripple effect, the circulation of good increases.

When we start our day, we can take inventory and think about the small acts of kindness we intend to bring to our world. We never know what others are dealing with in their lives. If we can bring even a small, but genuine, smile to their faces with our kind deeds, this helps fuel our own happiness. Smiles are contagious and smiles are something I like to catch and spread! The Dalai Lama provides a thought-provoking concept and practice. Every day when he wakes up he sets this intention: "*I am going to have kind thoughts towards others, I am not going to get angry or think badly about others. I am going to benefit others as much as I can.*"

Sometimes when we are going through dark days, we do not have the will or motivation to go out spreading sunshine. Though, deep in our hearts, we know that there are always a handful of good incentives to encourage kindness as a daily activity. Science has unveiled that going back to the fundamentals of life has positive outcomes for us. In fact, science has shown that acts of kindness facilitate happiness in the ones doing the kind act. Happiness and kindness release the hormone oxytocin, known as the "Love Hormone" or the "Cuddle Hormone." Oxytocin can cause a decrease in aging; it helps diminish stress, which fights aging.

With the increase in oxytocin, we have more access to our Prefrontal Cortex, also known as our executive functioning area of the brain, allowing us the ability to make more logical decisions. And if that is not enough reason to embrace kindness, science has also shown that kindness can offer a cardio-protective effect. This is because kindness helps to increase the release of nitric oxide in our system. Nitric oxide allows for the dilation of blood vessels leading to more circulation.

This is the same chemical that is released when we are sexually stimulated. And, who doesn't like that type of stimulation? Now, aren't these solid incentives to spread kindness every day? I certainly think so! May this be an incentive to bring the best version of ourselves forward.

In case you are wondering how you can manage to do this on a daily basis, here is my secret: (You can conduct an experiment and see what works for you). Every morning when getting out of bed, I smile. Yes, some days I have to force myself to smile. When I smile, my brain releases feel-good chemicals into the body, which helps to facilitate a positive start to my day. Even if the smile is forced, my brain doesn't know the difference, it isn't able to determine if it was a real or a fake smile. So, smile away! Begin every day with a smile and see if it impacts the outcome of your whole day. All of our physiologies are different; therefore, we do not all respond the same way. But it can't hurt to try this out.

When it comes to those around us, fortunately, or unfortunately, we cannot control what they do or do not do. However, we do have control over the things that WE bring to our day! The question is, how do we want to respond to life? When we allow our best selves to shine forward through sharing kindness, it creates a ripple effect! In the fantastic book: *The Five Side Effects of Kindness: This Book Will Make You Feel Better, Be Happier & Live Longer*, David R. Hamilton Ph.D. artfully illustrates the substantial positive side effects of kindness. He talks about the ripple effect: how one act of kindness can expand to positively impact people way beyond the individual who initiated the chain. Just like our smiles, our acts of kindness are also contagious. We have the power to initiate an immensely positive impact on the world, with just a simple act of kindness. I have heard and experienced numerous examples of how a single act of kindness opened unexpected new doors.

Here I will share the most recent experience that has already opened awesome doors for me and, most importantly, doors to new and wonderful friendships. This "random meeting" occurred while attending an amazing training workshop called DreamBuilder® hosted by Mary Morrissey and LifeSOULutions That Work, LLC: One of the 300-plus attendees was from Transylvania and I was intrigued and wanted to learn about her and her culture. Inspired to meet her, I went up and genuinely engaged with her by starting a conversation. I instantly felt a connection! We were able to connect again later that week and we had a great night talking and learning about each other's different paths.

During our conversations, I was intrigued by her, with all of her accomplishments, successes and the challenges she has soared above. In our conversations I was so impressed to learn she, Aura Imbarus Ph.D., has written a book: *Out of the Transylvania Night*, has been a guest on multiple television shows, is a professor, and she owns a print and online magazine called *See Beyond: Live. Love. Inspire*. Most exciting for me is that she knows two men whom I completely respect and who captivate me with their vast knowledge and work: Dr. Bruce Lipton and Dr. Joe Dispenza. I aspire to one day work with them in some capacity. I am enthralled with how people are placed on one another's paths. If you take the opportunity to engage and be open, you never know where a new connection may lead. This is an illustration of how kindness and connections can grant many unexpected gifts!

A study by Dr. Sonja Lyubomirsky Ph.D., et al. (2005) looked at doing five acts of kindness and the effects these actions had on our happiness. There were three groups: the control group, the group doing the five acts of kindness on the same day each week, and the group doing the five acts spread throughout the week. This study lasted for a period of six weeks. The results revealed that the group doing the five acts of kindness on the same day had significant increases in their personal happiness levels. Talk about a win-win formula! When we focus our five acts of kindness on the same day, we can help elevate our own levels of happiness.

In my view, happiness does not come from material items; it grows from meaningful connections. I do not care how fancy your car or home is; I care about you and your character as a human being. It is more vital for me to know what your heart is like. Are you generous or stingy? Do you smile or frown? Are you complimentary or critical of others? Do you take time out to play, dance, be silly and laugh, or are you a workaholic who is completely stressed out? These thought-provoking questions can help us gauge the level of happiness our connections bring. Attitudes and approaches to life affect those around us; they can also alter the chemistry in our bodies. These chemical changes have the power to bring positive or negative effects on our physiology. Being conscious of this helps us set boundaries around the type of people we allow in our lives.

There was up to a one in 500 million chance that any of us would be on this earth. Do you know why? There are between 30 to 500 million sperm released at a time, and you won the race! "*Let's face it, we all won the ovarian lottery*," said Alex Mandossian. You may not have been planned, but you definitely were not an accident. I want us all to think about this and know we are all born with a purpose and a gift. Some people have compassion, while others have humor. Some are strong leaders, while others teem with generosity. These qualities are what make us unique and they are gifts we can share with others in our attempt to give back to this world. Take a moment and ask yourself: "What are my strengths and how can I use them to improve my own as well as other people's lives?".

There is a secret code I share; it is P³. Used as a reminder, this secret code can be placed on your bathroom mirror, on your refrigerator or even as a screen saver. The meaning behind the secret code is P̲urpose, P̲assion and endless P̲ossibilities and we all have them. Do not allow fear to convince you of anything different. When we look at this secret code we can focus on our P̲urpose, P̲assion and endless P̲ossibilities, because we know that where our attention goes energy flows.

The older I get, the more I realize how imperative it is to be true to my heart and lead with my gifts. After all, this is what allows me to feel alive, to be in alignment with my purpose and passion and to live in peace. What's interesting is that I literally had to be knocked in the head twice to be able to find my path. I am not exaggerating. The details of these experiences will unfold later in the book. Every tragedy has a light or a silver lining, and we need to follow our heart's guidance to make the most of this life.

Just like everyone else out there, I was born with a gift. This gift is a strong ability to connect with people. I love people and love to hear their individual stories. My mother once told me that, starting at three years old, I would go up to strangers in restaurants and start talking to them. It is in my blood to have human connections.

At a young age, I was under the innocent impression that everyone was just like me: amiable, approachable, empathetic, and kind. Then somewhere during the "growing up" phase of life, I became cognizant of how wrong I was. Working at a large chain store as a pharmacy technician at the age of 18 really opened my eyes. That's when it hit me: people are not all the same. During my time there, I dealt with some very interesting personalities and not all of them were kind to me. I was over-the-top nice to people, even though I faced many extremely challenging personalities. Not realizing it at the time, this is where the understanding and experimenting with the impact of kindness started. Dealing with a ton of unhappy people at the pharmacy made me think, "Wow! How is it possible for some people to be so mean and angry?"

It was their prescription profiles and their medication history that gave me some insight. The medications on their profiles shared informative parts of their life stories. Many were trying to deal with some heavy circumstances in their lives; their medications created an illustration for me of the challenges they faced. My desire to fathom what was on their plates that made them so sour gave me the compassion needed to accept them for who they are.

My father was a pharmacist. He once said to me, "*Cyrina, try to remember your patients' names. They will feel more connected to you.*" Being in the same profession as him, I always took his advice seriously and applied it to my work. Thereafter I actively strove to remember the patients' names and small details about everyone in their family. I continued to treat each patient with courtesy, no matter how rude or mean they were to me at the beginning. As a result, most of my connections evolved to reach soaring heights. The patients went from yelling at me to sharing a smile, sometimes offering a hug, and even bringing thoughtful gifts, such as cookies they baked for me! The consistency in my behavior towards them created the shift. I knew their anger was not about me. Demonstrating that I cared about them and their families, respected them and was there to help them, facilitated a change in their attitudes towards me.

These interactions eventually allowed for many positive relationships to blossom. Genuine kindness goes a long way in creating positive and cordial relationships between people. I must confess I was not always successful in shifting people from the dark side and there were still some very challenging days. Many times, I had to take deep breaths and bite my tongue to stop myself from being rude or snarky. However, I can proudly say that my focus on being kind paid off in the long run. You choose your battles in life. And, to me, these battles were superfluous.

Approaching my service industry job as an obstacle course presented several new strategies. I embraced the fact that we never know what our day will bring. We are also subconsciously aware that it will have challenges, accompanied by a sense of accomplishment at the end of the day.

There have been times when I was browbeaten because a frustrated patient's prescription was not ready. Thankfully, knowing that there are choices, I decided to be as friendly as humanly possible. Most of the time, this sticky sweetness helped diffuse the situation, although not always. On the worst days, I would be yelled at repeatedly for things I literally had no control over. Sticking to my strategy to "kill 'em with kindness" usually delivered a positive outcome.

However, when I got home from a challenging day, I needed to blow off some steam! I cranked up some hardcore music, yelled the lyrics at the top of my lungs and danced my ass off to get rid of the negative energy I had absorbed during the day.

Fortunately, the bad experiences were counterbalanced with the times spent with thoughtful, kindhearted people, who were a joy to interact with, whenever they came to the pharmacy. When we develop an intuitive sixth sense, we can more or less anticipate people's actions or reactions. In fact, we know what to expect from them within the first few seconds. When we can decipher the personality of the person with whom we are interacting, we can steer the interaction by creating a positive spin and developing a connection.

Luckily, being an intuitive person has served me well in my personal, as well as professional, relationships. In fact, intuition is my secret to successful travel. My love for exploring new places has helped me connect with some phenomenal people across the globe. Often on my travels, I have met "random" people and ended up spending a day, or even in some cases weeks with them. I co-created wonderful shared experiences with them. Some of those people became life-long friends.

This is a classic example of how to embrace and live the philosophy of being in and enjoying the moment. It is what has given me the right mental frame with which to approach and to be part of this world without expectations. This lesson was learned through several extended trips around the world.

My mother attributes my travel bug to the love my parents had for travel. When my mother was pregnant with me, she and my father traveled extensively together. Since I was their first child, they figured that they should get their travel bug satiated before they were tied down with family responsibilities. My mom always mentioned how she wished she had a periscope to attach to her belly, so I could have peeked out to experience the places they saw, as they traveled the world. Nevertheless, life has been filled with travel adventures and "random" occurrences, which I look forward to sharing with you.

Hopefully, by now, you have an idea of the type of person I am, although as you read on, more will unfold. There's obviously a lot more to my life than the true connections with other people. I have been blessed to have an amazing family and many awesome friends! This path has been a diverse terrain that includes wonderful memories, remarkable relationships, unpredictable events, some disappointments, and countless illustrations of how interconnected we all are!

I like to say, *Your actions today may come back to bless you or bite you in the future. Be Aware!* This concept is something to think about and share with others. It is not just "The six degrees of Kevin Bacon" (the college drinking game). All of you are now three degrees from Kevin Bacon! One of my good friends, and former roommates, Bob Derosa, co-wrote the movie: *The Air I Breathe.* The five leading roles are filled with amazing actors, one being Kevin Bacon. I'm honored to know Bob and I must say that I am super impressed with my friend's accomplishments!

When we were in college, six of us lived in the same apartment with limited funds, but plenty of laughter. Bob Derosa was one of my five roommates. I feel honored to have played an extra in one of Bob's movies many moons ago. This has been my only acting gig to date. Bob is such an authentic guy, who has not let his success go to his head. I'm very proud of him and the person he has become! Since you never know what the future holds, do not limit yourself or those around you: always allow greatness and gratitude to grow.

Through a myriad of unusual personal experiences, I have been and want to continue to live my life to the fullest! I choose to be authentic, kind, happy and vulnerable. How are you allowing yourself to be happy and to enjoy this beautiful gift of life? My mission with this book is for us to ponder whether or not we are leading a life of purpose, based on a foundation of love, kindness, gratitude, and happiness. From there, we will go on a journey through a diverse landscape highlighting significant events in my life. I will share the influential lessons I have learned with the intention of encouraging you to enjoy your moments. So, buckle up, baby, and enjoy the ride!

Takeaway Lessons from this Chapter:

* ❋ Live in the moment!
* ❋ Be Conscious and Mindful in your day.
* ❋ Kindness and Happiness are beneficial in a myriad of incredible incentivizing ways.
* ❋ Being present with people opens unexpected magical doors.
* ❋ Remember this secret code: $P^3 \rightarrow$ Purpose, Passion and endless Possibilities. Where our attention goes, energy flows.
* ❋ "Your actions today may come back to bless you or bite you in the future, Be Aware!"
* ❋ "Always allow greatness and gratitude to grow."
* ❋ May we all Catch Happiness® through kindness and experiencing the ripple effect of our actions in our world!
* ❋ The most conscious connection created in this chapter of my life was feeling the connection to P^3 and the truth behind this secret code! This realization that we all have, Purpose, Passion and endless Possibilities was empowering and affirming for me.
* ❋ What connections were created for you in Chapter 1?

Chapter 2

Lightning Strikes!

Every human being has layers; some of us tend to look at others as one-dimensional without much depth. Often people are unwilling to spend the time to peel back the layers and find themselves living in a superficial world.

With aging, I realize we all have insecurities. I must admit it is a little comforting to see that insecurities run rampant in all humans and not just in me. At a young age, I lived under the impression that I was the only one who had insecurities and self-doubts. I now wish that a memo had been circulated early in my life with the information that all of us have some level of insecurity. None of us would have had to live with that frightening loneliness while believing that life is perfect with no insecurities for others.

Realizing that there will always be someone more or less beautiful, wealthier or less wealthy, happier or less happy and more athletic or less athletic than me made it clear that there is a spectrum for all human qualities. This was a light bulb moment! With that said, I am an overall confident person. Not because of how I look on the outside, but because of who I am on the inside. Honesty, kindness, adventurousness, authenticity, compassion, and empathy for others are traits that form the core of my self-assurance. You see, when confidence comes from the inside, it becomes easier to stand tall and feel proud, even if your exterior is not equal to that of the people surrounding you. To me, good character is always more attractive than an amazing exterior accompanied by a shallow interior and questionable character.

My insecurities, along with the collection of my near-death experiences will be mentioned throughout the book. This is obviously my perspective, formed by my experiences, plus avid reading and learning from stories of many who are on a similar path. While moving through my challenges, I have come to the realization that there are always positives along with the negatives in life. I continually strive to be my best self and have gratitude for the gifts that I have been given. We are all humans on this planet together. How will our choices affect the whole? My desire to share my story arises from my hope to offer some light and comfort to others, without them having to go through the challenging experiences I have encountered.

The true story of my journey has been full of death-defying events. By facing death three times, I have learned some essential lessons about happiness and having to reinvent myself, instead of giving in and giving up in the face of difficulties. My goal now is to educate and inform myself, as well as others, about the tools to Catch Happiness® in our lives and share them with the world! Events that have been called "tragic" forced me to confront the questions: "Why am I here? What is my purpose?" In my attempts to find the answers, I have been catapulted on a trajectory that has transformed my existence.

On my life's journey, I have encountered many obstacles and walls that have impeded my path as I tried to navigate my way around the unavoidable hurdles. I was obliged to reevaluate my life and reinvent myself. This was because ultimately, there were no other options. I either had to sink or to learn how to float fast enough to survive. Einstein said, *"Energy cannot be created or destroyed; it can only be changed from one form to another."* The walls placed in my way initiated the changes in the direction of my energy. This is what effectively led me to forge new paths for myself.

Now let's take a trip back in time to visit my ten-year-old self: a chunky, insecure little girl who, despite many challenges, was happy, always smiling and surrounded with lots of laughter and love. Let's just say, even though I was happy, the insecurity that came from being overweight started at a young age. At the age of ten, my family moved from the country club in New Smyrna Beach, Florida to the countryside in DeLand, Florida. DeLand was filled with many interesting and entertaining stories. The Bullards were the exact opposite of "The *Beverly Hillbillies*;" these city folks were going to try out life in the country! My parents no longer wanted to live in the golf course community. They were tired of being told, *"Your children are not allowed to leave their bikes outside in your yard."* The Country Club members wanted to keep the neighborhood as pristine as possible. We wanted to feel more free. So, we made the leap and moved to the country. This was a considerable and challenging transition, but one we were willing to embrace.

My parents bought a beautiful home with four bedrooms, two baths, and a den. We lived on five acres with the back 2.5 acres surrounded by a fence. These enclosed acres eventually became the home of our traditional farm animals: several chickens, goats, pigs, our pony named Sunshine, and a big tom turkey named Jerky Turkey.

Living in the country turned out to be an action-packed adventure filled with lively stories. About a month after we had settled into our new home, we decided to dive right in by purchasing a pig named Rosie. Instead of choosing to play it safe and start small with a few chickens, my parents jumped in fully and went big with a pig! We had little, if any, knowledge about the proper care of a pig; however, that did not stop us from adopting her. One day Rosie escaped from her pen. The escape resulted in the entire family (mom, dad, sister, two brothers and me) going on a pig corralling mission. This was how we met most of our new neighbors, as we ran through their yards trying to catch Rosie. We had no idea how fast a pig could run. I can say that we all got lots of exercise during the pig corralling days. As we raced our way through the neighbors' yards, we were cordial and very friendly with them. Today, I feel confident that our neighbors were thinking we had no idea how to live in the country.

My mother and I flew through the next-door neighbor's yard in hot pursuit of Rosie. As I ran, I was looking ahead of me but not at the ground. Suddenly, and before I knew it, my mother had swept me up in her arms. I had no idea how or why she swooped me up so quickly. However, the reason soon became obvious. Right in front of me was a Diamondback Rattlesnake, and I was about to step on it! My mom saved my life! At the age of ten, I was not exactly the lightest child. I was truly impressed with my mother's strength and the fact that she could pick me up so quickly.

To this day, I am still blown away by the strength my mother displayed that day. Several friends have said, *"Technically, Cyrina, you should add this event to your almost dying list."* However, after thinking about this suggestion long and hard, I decided to leave this event off the list. If I had been bitten or even had stepped on the snake, this event would have been included. In my mind, this incident is more of a close call than a near-death experience. This was more comparable to such an instance like when you swerve your car out of the way of being hit or when you slam on the brakes at just the right moment. I am thankful that my mom was present with me that day and that she helped save me from that snake.

This "Roundup Rosie" adventure, as I like to call it, was a different experience than we had initially predicted. We were under the naive impression it would take an hour or two and that we would catch her easily! However, it did not turn out this way. Before we knew it, it was day three, and we were still in hot pursuit! One of the neighbors came by, asking a simple question, *"Have you put out any food for the pig? Rosie will most likely come and eat out of the bowl."* ·

My slightly embarrassed parents had to confess that we had not yet tried this simple tactic to round up Rosie. We followed the suggestion, and wouldn't you know, Rosie appeared! She was on the back porch where we had left the bowl of food for her only two hours later. The Rosie roundup was finally successful! With this practical lesson, my family and I began to learn and grow, earning our country boots for the first time.

This was an interesting event in my life because we had several days of vigorous exercise. Plus, not only did we learn more about the environment of our new home, but we were also able to meet our neighbors in a very non-traditional way. This was the first team effort event we did as a family at our new home. We were able to laugh and make light of this somewhat embarrassing experience. Confident, we all learned that we could have fun and laugh about our shortcomings while gaining personal growth at the same time. Over the years, our farm animal collection grew, and we became savvier as we adapted to life in the country.

Being known as "The Pig Lady" at a young age was challenging and also embarrassing. Yes, I did suffer some consequences and trauma secondary to raising pigs and being overweight! Simultaneously, though, raising and showing the pigs at the fair was a huge learning experience. I loved those intelligent and fascinating little animals. My participation in 4-H helped me learn the skills needed to show a pig at the fair. I was intrigued by how I could use a cane and guide the pig in the direction I wanted it to walk, and train it to bow. It was amazing how quickly the pig learned to follow my lead.

Each spring, we would buy a little piglet, and raise and train it until it was time for the fair. Usually, raising the pig lasted anywhere between five and six months. I became very attached during that time to the pig because they're such sweet animals! This annual experience helped me receive scholarships and the money necessary to help pay for my college tuition.

"Pig Lady", the name used to describe me by a few not-so-kind classmates, was a challenge for me; it was one I didn't know how to respond to at that time in my life. I remember thinking at that time, "Why are people so mean?" Yes, I was overweight, although it was not by much. It doesn't matter how overweight someone is, making fun of someone is not helpful or constructive. It is appalling that people feel the need to be mean to others. Overweight people are very hard on themselves anyway and do not need anyone else to contribute to their negative self-talk. Offering resources to someone for their health is a much more constructive approach.

Feeling constantly bombarded and battered with negative talk, I grew to resent these two beautiful, skinny, and popular girls at school who were very critical and mean to me. One day, I'd had enough! Gathering my courage, I cornered the two of them and yelled, "Why are you so mean to me?!? You are no better than me and I do not deserve to be treated this way!" Yes, I was scared! But I knew I had to stand up for myself, as no one else was going to do it for me. It was illuminating to see that once I stood up for myself, they stopped being mean.

This made me realize that standing firm on our own two feet forces others to respect us. Thankfully, I learned this valuable lesson at a very young age and have now adopted the habit of letting myself stand tall, not allowing people to walk all over me. In retrospect, this was a huge step in my life. We must be our own best advocates and recognize that we, too, deserve to be treated with respect, while treating others with respect as well. This was my takeaway from being made fun of as a child. It allowed me to grow and stand up for myself, as well as being conscious of how I was treating others.

Let's come back to the story about my pig. When fall rolled around, there was a feeling of excitement, as well as sadness, this was the time when the county fair came to town. During this time I felt conflicting emotions. While I was excited to have the experience and opportunity of showing my pig, it was slightly traumatic for me to know I would have to sell the pig to a restaurant, grocery store, or a butcher. I learned to establish a rule for my family, we could not buy any pork from whoever had purchased my pig for at least one year after the transaction had occurred.

As a child, I was always understandably excited and proud about the amount of money I could make at the fair. Being eleven years old and able to raise $400 in 1981 was impressive. While showing my pig at the fair, the judges would rate its size, body structure, and ability to follow orders. They then auctioned off my pig to the highest bidder. During the following week, the company or business that had made the purchase came to our property and drove off with the pig. This was the state of affairs until a very traumatic event changed the regular course of these transactions.

I was in the backyard saying goodbye, when the men from the grocery store came to pick up my pig. As I walked away while the men lined up the truck, I heard a sharp noise. It was a gunshot! These men had the gall to shoot my pig on our property. Obviously, I knew that the pig was going to be killed; however, no one had ever killed one of my pigs on our family's farm. Given my young age, this event was bound to negatively affect my psyche. This was the first time I had to deal with the death of something I had dearly loved and helped to raise. Naturally, I was very upset and had become very attached to the pig after spending every day with it for months. Wailing with tears streaming down my face, I ran to my mother and she attempted to console me. Trying to calm myself down, I said to her, "I guess this is preparing me for when you die."

I had no memory of that part of the story until my mother reminded me of my words. I was angry with myself for saying such an inconsiderate thing to my mother. Not being a parent, I can only imagine how a mother would feel if her child had said something so cold to her face. To this day I still feel ashamed of my thoughtless statement. The experience of my pig's death was the first time I was made aware that life can be short and unpredictable.

The summer of 1982 was a very significant time in my life, as it was the year that I realized how fast things could shift and change. My siblings and I alternated chores. It was my week to feed our animals. It was a typical summer day in Florida. The sky was lit up and alive...beautiful with the bright sun and 90 plus percent humidity. Later in the day, the dark clouds started to roll in a very traditional Florida summer style. It is interesting to me how we can feel the temperature shift that precedes a storm.

This experience is the first on the list of near-death events in my life. I had fed all the farm animals and finished my chores for the day before the storm rolled in. Unfortunately, our dog was still in the fenced area. I yelled, "Puddles! Come on, Puddles!". However, he hadn't finished harassing the chickens and goats and was not ready to leave the grounds for safety. The sky became darker and the clouds kept rolling in as a storm was brewing. The atmosphere began to feel ominous as if something sinister lurked just beyond the horizon. With my arm resting on the fence, I waited for my dog. I couldn't leave him alone to fend for himself.

Suddenly, there was a furious bolt of lightning that filled the sky and surged down. It hit the fence and down I went. My right arm was on the metal fence which caused me to be indirectly struck by a huge jolt of lightning. I fell backward onto the ground and passed out. Getting up and feeling disoriented, I started to run as fast as possible. Later, I discovered that I had barely missed a board with nails sticking out of it, just one foot from where my head was when I fell.

Many different sensations were running through my body at that time. I remember feeling like the *Bionic Woman* from the 1970's television show. It seemed as if I was moving in slow motion, though I had never run as fast as I did that day. It was exhilarating to feel the electricity flowing through my body! Little sparks flying off my arms made for a very bizarre visual experience. My dad was in the front yard mowing the lawn. I screamed as loudly as possible, "Daddy! Daddy!"

Falling face-first into the bushes, I had spent all of my energy. To this day, I have a battle scar on my forehead to remind me of that moment in my life. When I became conscious, the first thing I saw was both of my parents hovering over me, crying in distress, clueless as to how long I had been passed out. Furthermore, I was unsure how I had traveled the 300 meters from where I remember falling to where my parents found me. To this day, I still have no memory of that moment in my life.

My younger brothers said they saw me crawling to the place where my parents found me. My father was the first to arrive. When he found me, I was face down. He rolled me over and saw that I was non-responsive.

Later I learned that my father held me in his arms as he called out desperately to my mother to come and help. She, fortunately, was certified in CPR and started to attempt to bring her daughter back to life. I was breathing within about one minute after she started CPR. Yet again, my mother had saved my life. This was one of the most emotional moments in my life and remains somewhat surreal, even after all this time.

My family also shared with me that they talked to me, trying to get a response for what seemed like an eternity. Finally, I responded experiencing intense physical sensation and a tremendous amount of pain. It felt like my right arm had been broken. Both my parents were health care professionals; my father was a pharmacist, and my mother a medical technologist. When it came to the right steps to take with their own child at risk, stress interfered with their logic. Finally, when I responded, they decided to drive me to the Emergency Room. They laid me down on the back seat. With my siblings in the back of the family station wagon, we went to the hospital. My father was driving, and my mother stayed by my side. They continued to talk to me en route to make sure I was still responsive. They were very present with me the entire time, and I am grateful for the sincerity of their love and their concern for me.

At the local Emergency Room, the physician on duty that day was Dr. Knight, he was a very nice man. My mom worked at this hospital in the laboratory and knew almost everyone in the ER. The ER staff took special care of me, as to them, I was Margie's daughter. Dr. Knight said to me, *"You are one lucky girl to still be alive, young lady!"* He then commented, *"Those flip flops you were wearing saved your life!"*

They were the old-style flip flops that had the rainbow colors on the side; they were what had grounded me and allowed me to live. Who would have thought those two pieces of rainbow-colored rubber on my feet, that probably cost around $2.99, would be one of the best investments we had ever made? They allowed me to continue my life.

My arm was still terribly sore. The X-ray showed that my arm was not broken - shocking considering all the pain I was experiencing. This proved to me that when lightning strikes, it packs a punch! The doctor decided to admit me to the hospital for monitoring. I was discharged the next morning and all seemed to be fine.

This was a unique experience. Statistically, the average human being has around a 1 in 100,000 chances of being struck by lightning in a lifetime. I happen to be one of them. Too bad those statistics haven't correlated for me and the lottery!

After this experience, my mother became, let's just say, slightly over-protective. Every time there was a lightning storm, she would gather us all up, as a mother hen would gather her chicks. Then, as per her instructions, the four of us had to stay huddled together in the hallway during the length of the storm.

For those of you who are not familiar with the weather patterns in Florida, let me tell you that the hallway bonding event was a frequent occurrence, as there was a lightning storm almost every day during the summer. My mother was being very protective and meant this ritual in the most loving way possible. However, this practice became a common recurring event in my childhood and went on for two years. Soon, we all knew the drill and became very familiar with that hallway in our home.

This experience illustrated to me that no one ever knows what the day will hold! A phrase by Bil Keane that resonates in my heart is: "*Yesterday's the past, tomorrow's the future, but today is a GIFT. That's why it's called the present.*" This statement makes me believe that we cannot change the past, nor can we predict the future (except for psychics). In other words, be grateful for the present. Most of us have heard this saying. It has been re-illustrated to me on multiple occasions. Hence, I believe in it wholeheartedly. Now, I am better at being in the moment than during my early years. When we don't live life in the moment, we lose part of our lives! When we are present and conscious of things that surround us, the gifts become more apparent to us.

On the other hand, when we focus on the negatives of life, more and more negative things arrive at our doors. Another quote that correlates to this is: "Everything is energy, and that's all there is to it. Match the frequency of the reality you want, and you cannot help but get that reality. It can be no other way. This is not philosophy. This is physics." Some say these are words of Einstein, while others refute this and say the words are from Darryl Anka and Bashar. Nevertheless, it is a thought-provoking statement worth sharing.

The cartoonist, Alex Gregory, created a very insightful cartoon about not being present. In his cartoon, a man while at work was thinking about golfing; in the second picture, the same guy was on the golf course thinking about having sex with his wife; and in the third picture, the guy was having sex with his wife, thinking about work. This cartoon illustrates how being present is a big challenge for many of us! We are missing out on thoroughly enjoying the moment, company, and experience to the maximum, simply because we opt out of being present!

Admittedly, with modern-day technology, it has become harder not to be distracted or to be drawn away by the smartphone every moment of our day. It is interesting and sad to see couples or families out to dinner all on their phones instead of interacting with each other. Often, I wonder if we have a more authentic, engaging experience if it would shift our level of connection with others. Wouldn't we create better connections if we learned how to value people more? Couldn't we also give of ourselves more generously, instead of dedicating so much time to a screen?

Being present is not easy! It is a challenge, one which must be taken up with courage and determination. I want to encourage you to allow yourself to be present as much as possible.

Start out by taking baby steps. Think of it as a science experiment, where you use yourself as the subject. When you are out to dinner, try asking the person or people you are with if they are open to participating in an experiment. First, try as a group to put away the smartphones. Make a rule to not touch your phone. Whoever fails the challenge first will have to buy everyone a round of drinks or desserts. This should give people some incentive or motivation, as well as add to the excitement for the experiment. In this way, challenge yourself and see how being present in the moment can affect your interactions, relationships, experiences, and happiness in a positive way. Plus, learn to say the word 'No' to non-mandatory events when you are feeling overwhelmed and have too much on your plate. When this is the case, being present is very challenging. I am sure that if you choose to apply this advice, you will find it life-altering.

In my own life, I have experienced feeling very loved by both of my parents, who, undoubtedly, would drop everything and be present to help and support me. My family, unfortunately, has had to deal with many different types of challenges. Naturally, as we have made our way through the thick and thin of life, we each have grown together. There are lessons to be learned in life. The lightning experience taught the Bullard family a few new lessons, but it is just one of the challenging events that my family and I share.

When I was 18, I lost my father. He was only 45 years old when he passed. He was younger than my age now. Although he will always be in my heart, the loss of my father was and still is very painful. With that said, I am very thankful to have had a great relationship with him. We would often, as a family, play foosball, darts, or pool. All of those times, we used to laugh hard and live fully without knowing that we were creating great memories. Memories of him serve as an anchor for me now. Was he a perfect man? No, I believe no human is perfect. But despite his human shortcomings, my dad was a good and loving man who had his issues, as we all do. I can say that I learned a lot about life from him. Losing my father at such a young age made me conscious of how important it is to be present with those you love and to live your life.

We all have lessons to learn. Many times, I have compassion for those who are distant or estranged from their biological family. However, "our family," is not necessarily our biological family. It can include the ones we choose. In fact, it can be composed of friends, significant others, and whoever else we want to invite and include in our "family circle." Feeling connected is essential if we want to bring together the pieces of this puzzle called life. Having these real connections helps to increase our levels of happiness. I encourage everyone to allow themselves to be open to connecting with others. Do this by being accessible and present for others on this journey. When all is said and done, this is what makes the ultimate difference in life.

Takeaway Lessons from this Chapter:

* Pigs run fast and are intelligent animals.

* Being in the moment is important and a gift.

* Making fun of people is not okay.

* We all have insecurities.

* Real connections are important.

* Change can be challenging and rewarding.

✳ The most conscious connection created in this chapter of my life was connecting with the strength inside and standing up to the two girls from junior high. This was a time when I was gaining the courage and insight to know that I can and will stand up for myself in my life.

✳ What connections were created for you in Chapter 2?

Chapter 3

Making Connections

Connection! What does that word mean? How does one truly feel connected? For me, this is an imperative question that must be answered in life. We know our connections create energy. What energy do we want to generate? Not just our connection with others, but also our connection to ourselves, our bodies, our environment, and our lives! We now know that feeling connected is part of what determines our level of happiness. There is also a non-traditional type of treatment prescribed by doctors in Europe that is gaining traction in other countries: Social Prescribing. This helps facilitate health and wellbeing through participating in different support groups in the community. This is an excellent tool to optimize our connections!

Passion, without a doubt, is a word that describes my love of travel. My passion lies here since traveling is one way that allows me to feel connected, not only with others and with the world but also with myself! I feel fortunate to have had the opportunity to take multiple extended trips around the world, experienced amazing adventures, and met some off-the-charts captivating people.

I will share a few fascinating events that have occurred on my journeys that made me realize the real power of connection between human lives. Although I traveled alone for the majority of my adventures, I never really felt alone. During my travels, unexpected people crossed my path who invariably changed my life. It was unusual for me to eat dinner by myself. I only ate alone on three occasions during one of my six months extended trips.

Wanting to embrace the moment is a strong desire of mine. Being present and experiencing the culture and its people during my travels was key. Because my father was so young when he passed away, it made me want to live life to the fullest. Meeting someone and spending an hour (or maybe twenty days) with them can be highly rewarding; you just never know how things will unfold. By keeping an open mind to the possibilities of serendipity and trusting our intuition, we will find things to celebrate in life.

Bali, Indonesia

At this very adventurous point in my life, I was backpacking around the world. My heart leaped with excitement when the plane landed at the airport in Bali, Indonesia. Having heard about this wonderful island, especially the beauty of the land and the people, inspired me to see everything that awaited me. While walking out of the airport, a British man and fellow backpacker, came up to me and asked, *"Hey, do you want to share a taxi into town?"* When backpacking, I was used to always being on a budget. So, I said to him, "Sure, why not?"

We hailed a taxi and began talking. He shared with me how his girlfriend was, unfortunately, unable to join him, so he was traveling alone. He seemed like a really nice guy with good character, so I trusted my intuition. He was open to possibilities and was all for trying out new things. Interestingly, the bonding time during the taxicab ride evolved into me staying in the same hotel room with him!

We slept in separate beds, and our relationship remained strictly platonic. For sure, my day was not turning out as expected. Starting from the shared taxi ride to sharing a room with a person who, until that morning, was a complete stranger is just one example of the interesting twists that would be placed on my path. Wondering where this would lead me, I remained curious.

The taxicab driver was a nice guy. He asked us if we would be willing to look at a timeshare. If we did, he would receive a $50 referral fee, which was a lot of money for him. So my new British friend and I decided to go to the timeshare the next day.

The timeshare property, of course, was beautiful! After we listened to the traditional 1.5-hour presentation, a salesman tried to rope us into buying. We had a great time joking with each other, saying, "Babe, remember the time we were in Vegas…" At that time, we had known each other for a total of only twenty hours! We laughed and made jokes with the salesperson, all the while pretending to be a couple. We knew we were not going to buy anything, but that didn't stop us from spending our time having as much fun as possible.

We continued to travel through Bali together, staying in the same hotel room or beach hut for the next fifteen days. We went to some amazingly beautiful places. (With that said, I am not sure there is any place in Bali that is not beautiful)! It was awesome to share the experience with someone! This British companion of mine, a graphic artist, had an eye dissimilar to mine; he saw the world in a different light. He helped me to open my eyes, showing me how to look at the world from a new perspective. For the first time in my life, I was able to see my surroundings and interpret my experiences through an artist's eye.

This man pointed out details to me about the colors of the Balinese traditional clothing and the ceremonies that we experienced together. Having a travel partner allowed my trip experience to expand in ways that I could not have predicted. It also showed and taught me more about Bali. We explored a shipwreck while scuba diving and attended a traditional Hindu ceremony. In short, we had amazing adventures together. Even though we have not spoken to each other since our time together in Bali, it was an unforgettable experience in my life. To this day I remember this time very fondly, it was a time when I felt connected and supported by this stranger who I now call a friend.

I feel confident that my experience in Bali with my British friend made my telomeres longer! You might be wondering what the heck are telomeres? Well, they are protective caps made of DNA and protein at the ends of our chromosomes. They protect our genetic data when cell division occurs. This may seem like an odd statement to make in the middle of a conversation about my vacation to Bali; however, I wanted to share some scientific information, along with my personal experience, in the hopes that it will expedite a healthier world.

A common way to visualize telomeres is to think of the aglet, the plastic tip on shoelaces. Telomeres keep chromosome ends from fraying and sticking to each other. They allow our chromosomes to be replicated properly during cell division. Hence, we want our telomeres to remain strong as long as possible to help slow down the aging of our cells. If our chromosomes are not protected, there are increased chances of getting cancer, cardiovascular disease, cell death, increased aging, and other various negative outcomes.

Therefore, optimizing our telomere length can help improve our cells, our bodies, and our overall health. In 2009, Elizabeth H. Blackburn Ph.D., Carol W. Greider Ph.D., and Jack W. Szostak Ph.D. won the Nobel Prize in Physiology or Medicine for discovering how telomeres and the enzyme telomerase help protect the chromosomes. *The Telomere Effect* is a very insightful book, by Elizabeth H. Blackburn Ph.D. and Elissa Epel Ph.D. This book teaches the science behind telomeres, as well as possible habits that we can adopt to have a positive impact on our telomeres.

Currently, scientists are showing us how our outlook on life can affect our telomeres. Researchers are comparing the effects of pessimistic and optimistic attitudes towards life on telomeres. It is really fascinating to learn that our thoughts can affect the health of our cells. After all, our thoughts are energy, and energy creates matter. Einstein gave us the equation $E=mc^2$ in which E is energy, m is mass, and c is the speed of light. We know that emotions are energy in motion. Now, think about this: what energy are we creating with our thoughts and emotions?

Once we have analyzed the impact of the energy we create and recognize how it affects our life and health, we can begin thinking about how to generate more positive energy for ourselves and our world. The psychologist, Aoife O'Donovan Ph.D., who works at UC San Francisco, studied the telomere length in postmenopausal women ranging from 50 to 86 years of age. She found through her research that the pessimists showed poorer immune system functioning (the system that helps fight infection), as well as shorter telomeres than people who were optimists. Thus, there is a correlation between our outlook on life and our physiology.

This information shows us that there are many different ways to look at the same situation. Likewise, there are many interpretations that can be deduced from a single event. Our perspective can have a potential positive or negative effect on our health. This is yet another layer to explore *"What is my intention for the day? How do I want to show up in the world today? How can I help myself and others to have more positive experiences?"* Hopefully, this kind of contemplation, now backed by scientific evidence, will help shift our thoughts and actions towards ourselves and others and create more optimism and positivity.

When it comes to emotions, it is imperative to express and release them effectively. Allow your feelings to have an outlet and give yourself a well-deserved present by refusing to stay in a depleted emotional place. There are many different ways to bring a shift in your life and deal with stress. I encourage you to find what works for you. You have a choice: will you implement what you have found to improve the quality of your life? Do you want to live a life you love or just exist? I encourage you to live a life of design, not one of default!

Dr. Dean Ornish, from UC San Francisco, demonstrated through one of his studies how lifestyle changes at any age can have a positive impact on the length of telomeres. He worked with two groups. The first group was the study group, which was asked to modify their lifestyles in terms of what they ate, their exercise, their stress management, and social support. The control group did not make modifications to their lifestyle. His study showed a 10% increase in the length of the telomeres in the study group, in comparison to a 3% decrease in the control group; this, in total, amounted to a 13% overall increase. This study indicates that it is never too late to introduce positive lifestyle changes to help improve the length of our telomeres. Dr. Peter R. Carroll states, *"Telomere shortening increases the risk of a wide variety of chronic diseases."*

This information provides a strong motivator to make modifications to our lifestyle. Dr. Dean Ornish said, *"Our genes, and our telomeres, are not necessarily our fate."* There are many stressors in our world, but how we deal with them is what matters. We are all different. The stress reliever that works for me may not work for others. Find what works best for you. Also, we need to be proactive and eliminate the stressors in our environment as much as possible. After we have done that, we can apply our newly acquired knowledge to our surroundings and manage the amount of stress we hold on to in our daily lives.

Here's a helpful suggestion: set the alarm every hour or so as a reminder to do a few minutes of deep breathing exercises. We live in a land of shallow breathers! The physiology of our lungs encourages us to take deeper breaths to bring more calmness. We know when we breathe shallow, we are activating the sympathetic nervous system receptors, which can give us an anxious feeling. When we breathe deeper, we activate more of our parasympathetic receptors, which will bring us more calm.

Take the time to look up a joke, to stretch, or take a brisk walk. There are other ways to hit the reset button; you have to find what works for you. A few minutes of a positive break helps you remain more focused, allowing you to be even more productive. I also encourage people to restrain themselves from going to their phones to scroll down to social media sites. Use your break time to allow yourself a few minutes of stress relief. This time should be reserved for feeling good about yourself, rather than adding to your anxiety by comparing your life to the highlighted reel of others' experiences, as you see them on social media.

I have just created this new technique for myself, and I love it!: I set the alarm for 33 minutes 33 seconds (yes, I am a numbers person). During this time, I shut off the ringer on my phone and try to stay as focused as possible on my work. When the alarm goes off, I set it again for 3 minutes 33 seconds; then I put on my headphones and dance to the music, drink some water or go to the restroom before getting back to work. Mind you, this is for when I am writing this book or doing other work for my business in my home. Make the modifications for what works for you and <u>your</u> environment. Hopefully, my practice gives you an idea of what you can do with your time.

Now, let's get back to Bali. The "random" meeting and time in Bali was filled with exercise, healthy food, and with the British man with whom I felt connected. The support I got made for a very positive, life-changing experience. I feel truly convinced that the time spent in Bali, lengthened my telomeres! My intention is to encourage you all to be present in your moments and to be willing to learn and expand. Seize the day and see where it takes you.

When I was 25 years old, I had an adventurous around-the-world travel escapade that could have ended very differently than anticipated! Five girlfriends, one being me, all pharmacists, decided to escape to Kiwi land. Three of us, including me, were Gators (University of Florida graduates), while the other two friends were alumni from a different university. I was very impressed with how well we all traveled together. Though the trip was extremely challenging, physically as well as mentally, we were thankfully able to get along well during our five-week journey together.

We rented a Pathfinder, which allowed us all to fit with our backpacks. The driver's seat was on the right side of the car, and this required shifting left-handed which felt very strange. We all alternated being the person behind the wheel; although driving needed to be a team effort. While driving on the left side of the road, we used to say, *"Left is life; left is life"* to remind ourselves to drive on the left side. On a few occasions, when we were the only ones on a small curvy road, we would all the sudden see another car coming directly towards us! Yes, it was our fault, as we were the ones on the wrong side of the road. We, therefore, learned how to react ridiculously fast. This made us pay attention to driving on a whole different level. I can proudly say that the award for the best team effort goes to the Penta Pharmacist group!

This adventure brings us to my second encounter on my list of life-threatening experiences. New Zealand is an amazing place to visit! It is known for its extraordinary beauty and the many adventures that it offers. We experienced hiking up and down beautiful mountains, trekking on the Milford Sound, a spectacular place. Caving in the Haggas Honking Holes was yet another experience that was totally out of this world! There we also abseiled down three waterfalls into a huge cave and rock climbed through small areas to exit the cave.

Blackwater rafting was another experience that we had - that's rafting down rapids on inner tubes. We wore our headlamps in a cave that was otherwise completely black. While we were rafting, we saw glow worms; this was something we had never even heard of before. It truly was a magical sight. This adventure provided all of us with a plethora of "first times." I highly recommend these activities to all of you adventure seekers and adrenaline junkies. These adventures will fill your adrenaline tank for a good long while.

Yet, it was the largest commercially rafted waterfall in the world - yes, in the world - that brought me face to face with my next life-threatening experience. First of all, I need to inform you that, as a group, we had all agreed ahead of time that we would not even think about participating in this 5+ grade whitewater rafting trip since it sounded insane. However, there was a shift, and a few days later, we were all in our wetsuits carrying a raft. I guess you can never say never; and no, these five pharmacists were not on drugs when making this decision. Though you may be thinking otherwise right now, we were all really pumped up and ready for the adventure to begin.

The guides gave us a briefing before we started on this adventure. They told us that there was a 50/50 chance that the raft would flip when it went down the 21-foot waterfall. Wow, the thought of the length of the drop was more than a little frightening. I had rafted before, but with a maximum drop of 5 to 6 feet, which with fast rapids gave you a rush of adrenaline and some fear. But imagine 21 feet, yikes!

We were all listening intently to the guides as they instructed us on the procedures to follow if the 50 percent flip occurred. If the boat flipped, the guide would turn the raft upside down. Your job would be to go under the raft, where you would find space to be able to breathe. In time, the guide would get everyone out of the raging waters. Now there was always the possibility that one person might be a lone ranger (the only one to fall out of the boat). If this happened, they knew that your first instinct would be to swim; however, that would be the wrong thing to do if you wanted to survive. Instead, they instructed us to allow our body to ball up which would change our surface area and we would be able to roll out of the rapids.

We had two guides in our raft; one manned the front and the other the back. I was in the back, seated right next to the guide for two reasons. First, I felt safe! Second, and more importantly, he had some pretty amazing muscles. I was positioned to take inventory of them and was completely psyched. We all started this adventure with the attitude of, "Okay, here we go! Game on!"

At first, there were a few mild, fun rapids that had only around 4 to 6-foot drops, so we were having a blast. When we got to a calmer area, the guides paddled over to an eddy and once again briefed us. Repetitious reminders were given out because we were about to embark on the craziness and these instructions were the keys to surviving this hazardous experience. They shared once again the importance of balling up to roll out of the water. The game was on once we were warned and ready to go. Off we went.

Holy moly! That was a huge drop with such a powerful rush of water. We got to the bottom, and I thought, "Oh shit, we got a 50 percent chance that our raft would flip!" However, the raft had not flipped. It very quickly became apparent that I was the only one to have fallen out of the raft, I was the Lone Ranger. This had become a whole different ball game, I immediately needed to change my plan of action. Alone, I was slammed with tons of powerful water. It was hard to catch my breath and, to top it all off, I was swallowing copious amounts of water.

A rather humorous part of this event was that my friends and I were all active people; out of the five girlfriends, I was the heaviest of the group. One would think that having a few extra pounds would help keep your larger rear in the raft! Soon I learned that was not a given, as I was the first and the only one to shoot out of the raft and into the furious water.

Beginning to panic, and you could tell because my first instinct was to try to swim in the wild waters. The instructors were right. Luckily, I was able to recall the briefing, and I told myself, "No, Cyrina, don't swim! Just ball up, and you will roll out," Thank God I was listening and paying attention to our guides. Yes, that tactic did work! I rolled out of that scary and forceful waterfall after what seemed like a lifetime of being stuck inside. It was then that I saw eight rafts positioned in a semicircle waiting to pull me out of the raging water.

The closest raft had a guide with dreadlocks, who said to me, *"I am going to pull you out, okay?"* I felt so overwhelmed after having swallowed about a gallon of water involuntarily during all of my flailings in the powerful waterfall. I was so exhausted that I had to lay there for a few minutes just to catch my breath! All of the people on this adventure started clapping for me and were happy that I had survived. Many asked me if I had seen Elvis, and I responded that I almost touched his blue suede shoes! That was an experience, for sure! Talk about cutting it very close!

The number of people who raft this insane, incredibly fun river per year is about 100,000, and of this large group, they say that one person dies each year. Thank God that in 1995 I was not the one to become a part of those statistics! A surprising part of this adventure was that we did not have to sign a waiver of any sort, which was slightly shocking to me, although things may have changed so many years later. On that same trip, when returning to America, I rented a boogie board in Hawaii; there, I had to sign an eight-page waiver. I can only marvel at the difference.

Through all of our experiences in life, we hopefully learn and evolve. From the awareness gained during my travel experiences, I learned to be open to the possibilities of "random" meetings, which may evolve into improbable experiences. I have learned that when I carry the emotions and thoughts of worry, anxiety, or anger, I miss out on the gifts this life has given me. Since we are all on different paths, the kind of impact that we have on our world depends on how well we respond to circumstances. Our thoughts and emotions not only affect us, but they also affect those around us. When we are stressed out, this energy is felt by others.

The bottom line is that we are all energy beings; our emotions are energy in motion. Understand that your attitude can make you approachable, or it can isolate you. Science has confirmed that creating meaningful social connections can have positive effects on our health, so it is important to learn how to optimize our connections in life.

It is always important to have a keen ear and to listen when instructions for escaping potentially life-threatening adventures are taught. Never forget to enjoy the moment and have fun on the journey, as you never know what the day will bring. Finally, remember to ball up and roll out of all literal and metaphorical life-threatening situations! These tactics can help you survive and live well!

Takeaway Lessons from this Chapter:

❋ Being open to random connections can bring fun adventure.

❋ Travel experiences are rich with unexpected adventures - so remain malleable.

❋ Emotions are energy in motion.

❋ Look for the positive in your day!

❋ Left is life!

❋ The most conscious connection created in this chapter of my life was with the random British man. This allowed me to trust my intuition and to create magical moments with the people placed on our path.

❋ What connections were created for you in Chapter 3?

Chapter 4

We Never Know

There are days throughout life that stand out. For me: May 29th, 2010, has huge blinking lights around it! That day had an enormous impact on my life. It was a beautiful day. I was in Vail, and it was the last day of my week-long holiday. Life was good! I was feeling very accomplished since I was putting my timeshare investment to good use. It was springtime in the mountains, and there are few places on earth that are more beautiful at that time. The picturesque scenery with the surrounding mountains, the beautiful flowers springing up all over the place, and the trees swaying with the wind: all of it made for a breathtaking sight.

Multiple friends had come up to visit and spend time with me in the mountains. We enjoyed our time together and created great memories that would last a lifetime. We went hiking and biking, we cooked dinners, and we spent a lot of time together "chillaxin". The view was spectacular from the condo patio. We gazed at the mountains while feeling the cool breeze from the clean mountain air and heard the birds chirp away. We even had a few birds come to visit us. I spent the last night of my stay alone and had a relaxing night; it was my time to unwind!

I woke up early the next morning to another beautiful, sunny day in Colorado. I wanted to experience nature and enjoy its abundant gifts. There really is nothing more captivating than nature in its full glory! I was drawn to go on one last bike ride to enjoy the magnificent day, before heading back down the mountain to Boulder. Geared up with those ever-so-attractive biking shorts and was ready to ride. The bike path chosen that day I had ridden many times before; so, I was very familiar with the twists and turns of the mild terrain.

I wish I could share with you that I was mountain biking off a cliff like a pro; but, I am not one to embellish stories. I was on a road bike on a smooth-paved path. So here I go! This is my best memory of the day on which the third, and hopefully, the final experience of my collection of life-threatening events took place. On that spectacular morning, I took in my surroundings as I biked on the beautiful path. On my way back to the condo with about half a mile to go, my day took a sudden shift. Something went horribly wrong and my memory stops there….

On that day, I was 39 years old and was about to be met with events that would forever change my life. This moment made a huge impact on my life. It forced me to discover many new things, learn many life lessons, recognize the need to embrace change, and to be present in the moment. I was alive! This event not only had a huge impact on my health, physical and mental, but also on my spirituality. Honestly, it made me question my purpose in life. This event encouraged me to listen to my intuition by paying attention to the obstacles, opportunities, and signs placed on my path; all of these focus light on my purpose. As I mentioned earlier, I had to be knocked on the head twice, quite literally, to have the light bulb of understanding go off. But, I'm still here on this fantastic life-changing journey!

Thankfully, during this life-altering bike ride, my helmet was on my head. If it wasn't, I would not be here today. The bicycle ride that day was not extreme by any means. This ride could have been easily accomplished on a cruiser bike. Many days I see a family out on a bicycle ride, a wonderful activity for a family to do together. The children, thankfully, are all geared up with helmets; however, the parents are often not.

I am not sure of the logic behind the inequality of helmet safety on such a family outing. In the case of an accident, if the children are fine but their parents are severely injured, would the children be able to take care of their parents, or even themselves? I feel very strongly that adults must lead by example. What do parents teach their children when they do not follow their safety instructions by not wearing their helmets? Isn't it practically the same as saying: when you're little, you have to wear a helmet to protect your head, but when you are grown up, you no longer need to protect your head? PLEASE wear your helmet...always!

Yes, some people might not find the sight of their head or hair under a helmet particularly cool or flattering. However, shouldn't they think about the potential consequences of not wearing a helmet? With that said, I am very thankful that we live in a country where we can all make our own choices. I may not agree with others' decisions or opinions, but I respect that they have a choice to do whatever they decide to do with their lives.

Mark was the lucky soul who witnessed my entire accident; he rescued me, or you could say that he was my first responder. I'm confident his day did not exactly go as he had planned. He was driving to the post office and saw my accident. I am so grateful that he was there and that he was willing to help me. When he stopped to check on me, he soon realized that I was non-responsive. Fortunately, he had been trained in CPR and began to work on me. There was also another gentleman who stopped to help; I do not know his name, but I am very grateful to him, as well! Thank you, my mysterious lifesaving responder.

Mark called 911. The dispatcher was calm to the point of dismissiveness and said something to the effect of, *"Oh, just a bike accident!"* Mark was very firm and made it known that I was in a very critical state and needed help immediately. The ambulance arrived, and I was taken to Vail Hospital. There, the team worked on me while waiting for Flight for Life®. I was transferred to the helicopter and was en route to Denver Health, a Level 1 Trauma Hospital, located in the heart of the city. To this day, I have no recollection of that time on the path near the post office, the ambulance, the helicopter ride, or the next 18 days of my life! Yet, this $26,000 helicopter ride was well worth every penny. Thank God for insurance!

If you do not believe in God or a higher power, I respect that. However, I would think there has been a time or two in your life when your intuition kicked in and guided you. Or, there are those times when you think, *"Why is this opportunity presenting itself to me?"*. Oftentimes there are no rational answers for things that happen in our lives. Sometimes, my belief in God differs from that of many people in my life. But despite our differences, we have respect for each other. Many of them do believe that we are energy beings and can feel the energy of other people.

My friends and I often joke and say, *"Wow! Did you feel the energy from that person?"* Now, this energy can be positive or negative. Someone who has great energy is the person whom we all want to hang out with. On the other hand, some people have very negative energy that is very draining. You feel a lack of vitality when you interact with these energy vampires. Naturally, you do not want to be around such people, at least not that often. My friends also believe in the magical word 'serendipity,' which is officially defined by Oxford as the *"Occurrence and development of events by chance in a happy or beneficial way."* My belief is that God is placing these magical moments or opportunities on our paths and that the more gratitude we have the more of these magical moments will continue to appear in our lives.

On the day of my bike accident, the last friend I had spoken to on my cell phone was Cella. Therefore, she was the one Mark called to let her know what had happened. Cella is a pilot, who at the time of the call, was about to take off on a flight. She called our mutual friend, Tyre, who started contacting everyone. Tyre's hard work allowed for many of my friends to be present for me when I arrived at Denver Health! So grateful that I was supported by the love and efforts of my family and friends.

Furthermore, I have no memory of my time at Denver Health and can only share with you the information that I have been told. When I arrived at Denver Health in the helicopter, friends were waiting for me. After landing, I was quickly taken to the ER and stabilized. This was a very long process, and things did not look good for me; the prognosis was not favorable. My mother, who lives in Florida, was contacted. That day she proved that when you are a mother, you make the impossible possible. She became supermom once again! She threw clothes in a suitcase and had a friend drive her to the airport. She arrived in Colorado on the same day as my accident. She was in mission mode.

Dan, who was a mutual friend of my mother and mine, picked her up at the airport. He "happened" to be in Colorado, although from Austin, Texas. He was visiting his sister in Denver. Dan and I were supposed to join my friends in Boulder and run the 10 Kilometer Bolder Boulder race together. Later, Dan told me that he drove like a bat out of hell, at about 90 miles an hour, to get my mother to me as quickly as possible. He was shocked that he did not get a speeding ticket. Thankfully, Dan was there and was willing to help. It was comforting for my mother to have someone she knew to pick her up at the airport during this challenging time.

My family walked into a scary situation, where the potential outcome was very uncertain. They were not even sure if I would survive this accident. My state was very critical; it was one day, or one moment, at a time. They shared with my mom that I had suffered a DAI TBI (Diffuse Axonal Injury Traumatic Brain Injury). In layman's terms, this was a shit ton of damage to my brain. And not only that, I also crushed the T-7, the thoracic vertebrae 7, which is located in the center of the spine.

According to Wikipedia, Diffuse Axonal Injury is: *"A brain injury in which scattered lesions in white matter tracts, as well as gray matter, occur over a widespread area. DAI is one of the most common and devastating types of traumatic brain injury and is a major cause of unconsciousness and persistent vegetative state after severe head trauma. It occurs in about half of all cases of severe head trauma and maybe the primary damage that occurs in concussion. The outcome is frequently coma, with over 90% of patients with severe DAI never regaining consciousness. Those who do wake up often remain significantly impaired."*

After reading this, a thousand thoughts ran through my mind! I felt extremely blessed, I realized that there was a lot more that I had to accomplish in my life.

The following are my mother's words, which relay her perspective for this time in our lives: *"Cyrina's accident occurred on a Saturday afternoon. It was May of 2010, and I had just come into the house when the phone rang. It was a phone call from one of Cyrina's friends, Jen, telling me that Cyrina had suffered a road bike accident. She told me that the hospital Cyrina was being seen at was in Vail in the mountains and that they were sending her to Denver. I thought I would wait until she was evaluated and in a bigger hospital before traveling from central Florida to Denver. Less than ten minutes went by before I got another phone call; this time, the tone had changed. The situation was very serious, as Cyrina had a head injury, I was asked to come as soon as possible.*

By divine intervention and with help from family and friends, I was able to arrive at Denver Health in about 5 hours. After arriving at Denver Health, I was led to a crowded waiting room, which was full of young people who were friends of Cyrina. Her close friends attempted to inform me of what happened. My mind was full of confusion as to what and how this could happen. I could tell that her friends, who were doctors and physician assistants, knew the prognosis of this injury and that it was extremely grim. As I entered her room, I could see my daughter; I had never seen her so still and restrained. The reality of her being on a respirator, IVs, and tubes was horrible to see. I desperately begged God to take this foreign reality away.

How could my strong, athletic daughter be hurt this seriously from falling off a bicycle? They told me she had been wearing her helmet and it had broken into three pieces. That evening, after the waiting room cleared, I decided to stay back at the hospital. My fears would not let me leave the area. What if something happened during the night? Cyrina was all alone, and I needed to be there if she awoke. I was full of questions, and I was afraid to think of those what-ifs that ran through my mind. I was in this empty space where the control of my daughter's life was not in my hands. I felt desperate.

In the morning, I decided to find a church service at the hospital and pray and speak with the pastor. My hopes were pinned on God's help, the skilled medical staff, as well as Cyrina's exceptional ability to accomplish what she sets out to do. She might live. Please let her live, God! Two days later, on Monday, the family gathered in Denver. We were summoned to hear the reports of CT scans, X-rays reports, and a treatment plan from a host of doctors in white coats. The neurosurgeon explained that the injury was severe; she had suffered a bleed called a diffuse axonal bleed of the brain.

The trauma to the head had ripped the axons apart, which caused extensive bleeding in the brain and down in the brain stem. Other injuries were a break in the occipital condyle bones at the base of the skull, broken ribs, and a burst fracture of the T7 vertebra. The orthopedic surgeon stated that the condition could cause permanent paralysis of her body. He suggested a molded body cast and recommended to hold off surgery due to the severe condition of her brain and neuro-responses. I felt sick inside when they told us that she may never be independent again and that it was unlikely that she would be able to work as a pharmacist and function as she did before.

The trauma team of doctors told us not to look up her condition on the internet. Processing this information made me stop; the process of taking a breath changed from being unconscious to a conscious one. I used to spend long days at the hospital. I was totally absorbed with Cyrina's struggles and spent all day just getting through the traffic of nurses, respiratory and physical therapists, and doctors. All of this was exhausting for Cyrina. The demands being made on her body to survive seemed overwhelming.

I needed something to hold onto to give me direction and hope. I found it! Soon after, things seemed to settle down for me. John 14:1 spoke loud and clear: "Do not let your heart be troubled, trust in God and in His Son." Releasing her to God was the very best prayer; I felt Jesus had heard, and I was comforted. I used to spend long days at the hospital, and I remember, when I arrived, I would go to her left side. This was her active side; I would touch her and tell her I loved her. I tried to hold her hand, so she would not pull out her IV.

I don't recall when she started to remember my watch. Cyrina would spin the watch, look for the clasp, unlock it and lock it and spin it around. These actions told me to keep hoping that her brain was functioning. Days went by. I wasn't sure if she knew who I was, till the day she opened her eyes and looked at me. She touched my face and said, "Mom." When I looked into her eyes, I felt tears of joy and relief come to my eyes."

This was what my mom felt during those long, endless days before I regained consciousness. I'm very thankful to have a mother who is such a strong, supportive, and loving person! The doctors told my family that they would most likely have to take care of me for the rest of my life. Life sure can change in a second! The doctors also warned against me becoming overstimulated; they asked for the energy in my room to be kept as positive and calm as possible. My family was very selective in who they would allow into my room because of the need for positive energy. Apparently, the waiting room was filled with my friends and I always had love, positive energy, and prayers surrounding me!

One of my dear friends, Neide, who is an ER physician, did her residency at Denver Health. She knew many of the doctors and nurses who took care of me. She was able to help my family navigate and connect on another level with the doctors and nurses. My friend is one of the nicest people you will ever meet. Also, she has a wonderful relationship with many of the people at Denver Health. My brother, Jason, who lived in Boulder, came down to support me and to be with our mom. My sister, Malena, and my gay husband, Rob (I will explain later), were on the same flight the day after my accident. My other brother, Justin, and his partner, Tim, arrived; meaning that my entire immediate family was there.

I have such a loving family and amazing friends. They were all there to support me and each other. I had no idea what was going on at the time, though I'm confident I was feeling their love, even while unconscious. Thank God for Western medicine. Some people may not feel comfortable with the term "miracle." Maybe an outlier, the unexplainable, or a medical mystery would make some feel more comfortable. Regardless, we know these events and experiences exist. In my heart of hearts, I believe my recovery was a true miracle.

I would like to give a loving suggestion here: there is a spectrum in life that tells you that things are not black and white. There is often a lot of grey in most situations. We need to allow patients and their families to know both sides of the spectrum when dealing with any situation. My family and I are extremely resilient people and were able to defy statistics and the doctor's prognosis. If I had not been a resilient person, their prognosis could have become a reality, and my family would have had to take care of me for the rest of my life. I'm confident that God played a huge role in my recovery.

If the doctors were to give a poor prognosis early on, people who are not resilient would start to believe that this would be their reality. There is a potential spectrum for any prognosis; I suggest that the medical world consider and share both sides of the spectrum. With this said, I do not want to sugar-coat shit. Yes, there is the potential of a severely limiting prognosis. But, at the same time, there is also the potential for a miracle, medical mystery, or an outlier. It is respectful and empowering to allow the patient and their family to be able to radiate positive energy and to hope for and envision the most optimistic outcome. Fortunately, I had amazing doctors, nurses, therapists, and other medical staff with my resilient family by my side. I would like to encourage the medical world not to put limitations on people.

If the loving members of the patient's support system are encouraged to hold on to the potential of an optimistic outcome, their thoughts become more positive, hopeful and powerful. Thoughts are energy! Remember, $E=mc^2$. Please allow both sides of the spectrum of the prognosis to be known, for the patient and their families so that they can see some light.

We are all energy beings having a human experience. Thus, we need to allow ourselves to think about how our energy affects other people, our own lives, and our health. I believe Napoleon Hill, who said, *"Whatever the mind can conceive and believe, it can achieve."* The power of prayer is an incredible source. If you do not want to call it prayer, I encourage referring to your actions as sending love and positive thoughts or energy in the direction of the intended person. This has only positive effects and has no side effects. Have you ever noticed that if you have a negative attitude, there seems to be a sequence of adverse events that occur in your life?

As I mentioned earlier, in my life, the opposite holds true; when I express gratitude and have a positive outlook, life seems to be in flow. The more expressions of gratitude I make, the more likely I can see the positives in life instead of the negatives. Both of these are indeed in our lives; the question is, what do we want to focus on? This has been a fascinating process to witness. Science shows we are happier when we express gratitude. However, you have to find what works for you. My observations in the world of science confirms that being grateful can help bring more happiness to our lives. Dr. Sonja Lymbomirsky did a study and found that writing down five things you have gratitude for once a week over a period of six weeks brought more happiness. This is not a lot of time to dedicate to writing down what you are grateful for in your week with the potential for positive outcomes! The increase in happiness you feel is well worth the small investment of writing down your gratitude!

Returning to my 18-day coma, confined to bed and not conscious. Apparently, I did talk, although making very little sense, if any, with zero memory of this time. I'm very confident that the love, positive energy, and sensory stimulation (touch, music, loving words) paved the path that had a positive impact on me, my healing process, and my journey. My family was entirely focused on a few things: They allowed only positive energy in my room and played calming music for me. My friend, Marisa, who is also a physician, read to me and touched me by putting lotion on my hands. Many people said loving things to me, even though I was unable to communicate with them.

An ex-boyfriend, who lived out of state, contacted my family to see if he could visit me in the hospital. Although he was coming from a loving place, my family did not know how this would affect me, so they did not allow him to visit. They were very conscious of the potential disruption of the energy they were trying to create and maintain in my room. I am not able to mention everyone who played instrumental roles by being helpful, loving, and supportive of my family and me, but all of those people know who they are. Thank you from the bottom of my heart, sending big hugs to you all!

At the time of my accident, I owned a home with one of my best girlfriends, Jen. Jen was married and lived with her husband during this time. She had rented out her room in our home to Melissa. My mother is a huge fan of Jen's because she is a very hard-working, level-headed, and calm person. Jen stayed very connected with my family and was at the hospital as frequently as possible. Melissa, my housemate, was welcoming to my family and invited them to stay with her. She was very helpful through the process and helped to get all the things that needed attention accomplished. Terri, a good friend of mine, and also of my sister, let people stay at her place which helped things to flow easier.

Gifts arrived from all over the world for me. Friends' children drew and painted pictures and sent their loving art to me. Friends would send poster boards with photos and captions about our times together. I received all of these beautiful pictures filled with love, although I did not get to enjoy them until later.

Another generous gift came from Ali and Debbie, great friends of mine, who organized a system to have friends cook dinners for my family. When I was able to process this extremely kind act, I was deeply touched by how lovely everyone was to my family and me during this difficult time. My neighbor, Luke, was generous with his time and mowed my lawn. This journey of mine was a true team effort.

An outlier in my care was my intuitive healer. Before this situation, I had not a clue about intuitive healers. My intuitive healer, Trevor Hart, was a key player in my healing process. The night after my accident, my friends of 15 years were allowed to come into my room. My family, as mentioned earlier, was very selective of whom they would allow to visit. Zoe and Dennis were welcomed. This story, I feel, serves as a sign that there are no accidents, and there are divine interventions in life.

Fascinatingly, just three weeks before my accident, my sister visited Denver; she had recently gone back to school to become a massage therapist. Because Zoe has been a highly-skilled massage therapist for years, I really wanted them to meet. At that time, I shared with my sister what an important person Zoe was in my life! Before that meeting between Zoe and my sister, my family had never known what important people she and Dennis are in my life. That meeting permitted their entrance into my hospital room.

Both Dennis and Zoe are very spiritually connected. After their visit to the hospital, they felt the need to call Trevor, the intuitive healer, to hire him to work on me. They shared with me that Trevor never answers the phone on the first call, but he did that night. Trevor started working on me remotely immediately with Zoe and Dennis's help. After two sessions, Zoe and Dennis contacted my family to see if they wanted to continue with the sessions for me. Like me, everyone in my family is science-based, no one in my family had ever heard of an intuitive healer. My sister and I are pharmacists; both of my brothers are engineers; my mom is a medical technologist. And as I mentioned earlier, my father was a pharmacist.

As a group, my family made a shared decision to continue the sessions with Trevor. They did not want to have any negative impact on my healing process. Trevor knew what was going on with me, and he undeniably had an impact on me and my healing. My sister met remotely with him via the phone to help with my recovery. Malena said it was amazing how many details Trevor knew about my situation with her sharing only very little information with him. I asked Malena to write a bit about her experience at that time with Trevor, to shed some light on the impact he made.

Here are Malena's words: *"The first I heard of Trevor Hart, an intuitive healer, was from my sister's friends Zoe and Dennis. Zoe is a massage therapist with a background in alternative and energy healing therapies. After seeing my sister, unconscious and lifeless in the ICU bed attached to a ventilator, I knew we had to seek out every complementary healing modality in addition to the traditional Western medicine practices. Within a couple of days of my sister's accident, I contacted Zoe and Dennis to learn more about Trevor Hart and his skills. Zoe and Dennis highly recommended Trevor and felt very strongly that he could help Cyrina. They had even paid for two remote healings with him.*

From then on, I had phone sessions with Trevor at least once a week – sometimes twice a week – for at least two months, spanning Cyrina's critical ICU stay, traumatic brain, and spinal cord injury rehab and through her spinal fusion surgery. I would take detailed and lengthy notes about Cyrina's medical condition and treatment every day and then share this with Trevor. He would use this medical information and ask me questions about Cyrina to guide his remote healing sessions on her. I never met Trevor, nor did he ever meet Cyrina while she was hospitalized. Also, I chose to keep these remote, healing sessions private; my family knew about them, but the medical team had no idea.

Trevor always asked me what Cyrina's greatest healing obstacle was for that week and used that as the focus for his session. For instance, while Cyrina was non-responsive and on a ventilator in ICU, she developed pneumonia and needed to be on IV antibiotics. I asked Trevor to focus on clearing her lungs of this infection, and within 24 hours, her health improved dramatically. Trevor incorporated Western medical anatomy and physiology terminology with Eastern philosophies when describing Cyrina's health and well-being. He always spoke of her constitution and will to live in percentages and remarked that they were extremely high for someone in such a dire medical state.

Speaking with Trevor was therapeutic for me and gave me hope that my sister would not only recover but have a quality life! During our conversations, I was amazed at his insight and intuition about what was going on with Cyrina medically. I could not explain, but I felt Trevor was helping my sister get better and stronger to the point that she ended up exceeding all expectations we had regarding her recovery!"

May Malena's words give you some insights into the benefits of complementary healing techniques that are available to us. We are forever learning as we are being exposed to different types of healing modalities. Dr. Joe Dispenza is someone I completely admire and follow his teachings. He offers alternative healing modalities and has a vast knowledge of neuroscience, epigenetics, and quantum physics. I had the opportunity to see him speak in person in the fall of 2018, and I was very inspired and impressed by his knowledge and the remarkable results seen through his teachings. We need to allow our circle of healing modalities to expand and encompass the right technique for our individual situations.

When we feel supported, we are more likely to have a better sense of well-being. My friends and family were endlessly supportive in many ways; they even started a *CaringBridge®* page to help keep people updated on my progress. *CaringBridge®* is a supportive resource; it facilitated decreasing the number of calls and emails with questions about how I was doing to my family. Friends from all over the world wrote such beautiful entries on the page. The doctors were highly uncertain about whether or not I would survive this severe injury. The potential prognosis gave everyone the impetus and license to write and speak the truth, as my friends shared their feelings for me from their hearts.

Why does something so traumatic have to happen to allow us to speak from the heart? My family read me the entries left by my friends and relatives, even though I was still in a coma. Without a doubt, I was able to feel the positive words and energy contained in these loving messages. I feel the need to encourage everyone to speak from their hearts. This is an intelligent part of one's anatomy that can bring another layer to any relationship. Being real and true to your heart can allow your connection with people to expand, deepen, and grow. Warning: if you like superficial relationships, do not speak from the heart.

This also leads me to delve into epigenetics and optimal healing environments. Epigenetics is *"the study of changes in organisms caused by modification of gene expression rather than alteration of the genetic code itself."* according to the Oxford Dictionary. DNA modifications are not occurring at the sequencing level. The change is with the effects on the gene activity, whether they are turned on or off. I find this so fascinating! We cannot control the DNA we are dealt, although we can control many factors in our environment. We see these effects when we are in utero, as this environment has a physiological impact on us before we are even born.

This, I feel, should be shared with every expecting parent, with the hopes that it will encourage them to try to create a loving relationship from the beginning. Also, encouraging eating healthy food and keeping the environment as positive as they can. When the mother is stressed out, the fetus is also exposed to cortisol (the stress hormone). We now know that when we are stressed, the blood flow to the prefrontal cortex area of the brain is decreased and given to other areas of the brain, for the flight, fight, or freeze response. The same also occurs for the fetus, which can ultimately affect the development of his or her brain.

My environment, during the coma, was as positive as it possibly could be. My girlfriend, Marisa, who is now a doctor at Denver Health said she has never seen that many people in a waiting room for one patient. The prayers, love, and empowering energy sent my way by all the friends, family, and acquaintances had a fantastic impact on my healing process! Even though someone is in a coma, they are still energy beings and can feel the energy around them. The positively charged environment in my room had a soothing impact on the outcome of my severe and critical situation. We did not do a study, and I have no scientific data to back this statement up, although I fully believe from my heart that this is the truth.

Denver Health took outstanding care of me. It is a great hospital for a patient who has suffered a Level 1 trauma. I have zero memory of my time there, although my friends and family have very positive things to report and share about Denver Health. With my positive healing progression, it was time for me to say goodbye to Denver Health. Please join me as we travel to the next stop on my journey; presently, we are in transition to Craig Hospital.

Takeaway Lessons from this Chapter:

* Helmets are important and saved my life.

* Stopping to help someone could save their life and be good for our hearts.

* The support and love given by family and or friends to a person dealing with challenges will experience benefits.

* The environment we surround ourselves with can have an impact on the expression of our genes. Epigenetics, a fascinating science, confirms we need to be conscious of our surroundings.

* Our acts of kindness can have the potential to create a huge ripple effect and allow more positive energy in our world.

* I am sharing this information with you to have people realize that their support and positive thoughts can have an impact. Encourage anyone who has a friend or family member who is going through a hard time to please allow themselves to feel loved and supported. The acts of kindness and support can have a positive effect on them and their mindset. We can all help each other out, as long as we are coming from a loving place.

* We know through science that renewing or depleting energy in your environment can have a physiological effect. We, fortunately, or unfortunately, cannot control anyone else's actions; we can only control what we do. What energy do you want to bring to this world? Later I will share how to help people Catch Happiness® through kindness and the ripple effects that you can have on others, yourself, and our world through simple acts.

* The most conscious connection created in this chapter of my life was feeling connected to the energy surrounding me. Without a

doubt, while in a coma I know that the love and support surrounding me was instrumental in my healing.

❋ What connections were created for you in Chapter 4?

Chapter 5

Craig Hospital

Opening my eyes, I felt very disoriented. I looked down and saw myself lying on a gurney in an ambulance and thought, "What in the hell is going on?" Luckily, I saw and recognized my mom, which gave me a sense of calm, safety, and comfort. This was my first memory, since that life-changing event in the mountains. In my state of disorientation, I was under the impression that I was in Florida, where my mother lived. I recall asking my mom, "Are we going to Daytona Beach?" We were not in Florida, we were en route from Denver Health to Craig Hospital.

Craig Hospital is a world-renowned hospital that specializes in the care of patients with Traumatic Brain Injuries and Spinal Cord Injuries. During this time of my journey, you can imagine that I was under a lot of strain. Despite this, I tried to bring laughter and lightness to this challenging and somewhat surreal time in my life. A common joke I share now is, "To be a patient at Craig Hospital, you either had to have a TBI or a spinal cord injury. I had both requirements! What an overachiever I am!" This was the most mentally and physically challenging process I had experienced in my life.

This time was filled with uncertainty, concentrated care, focus, effort, hard work, and a lot of prayers. This intense and draining period of my life fostered a positive outcome with exponential growth and recovery! Fortunate to have had an amazing team helping me navigate through this time successfully. The team included: doctors, speech, physical and occupational therapists, nurses, and the medical staff. I felt very connected to my health care providers, and they were definitely on my side. They were part of my team and on a mission for me, to optimize my recovery and my life.

My sister was my right hand and one hell of a Rock Star advocate. Many of my doctors would share with me that my sister made sure they were doing their job right. As I mentioned before, my sister is also a pharmacist, and she is very meticulous! She did tons of research and spent hours making sure I was getting optimal treatment and care to ensure the best possible outcomes for me.

You should see the volumes of notebooks she diligently filled with important information. The notebooks are filled with different colors of ink, and her notes were extremely detailed. These notebooks were a true illustration of all the work and effort Malena did for her injured sister. She, unlike me, is very attentive to details and is also extremely organized. I often joke and ask her why she got all those genes! I am forever indebted to her for her love, knowledge, hard work, and encouragement!

My environment and surroundings were always in the process of becoming optimized by my family. While at Denver Health, and now at Craig Hospital, they were very protective of me. They were always cautious about what energy they allowed around me. For that reason, they filtered a lot of the information. This was their way of allowing me to have the most optimistic view possible about my future and not to be limited by an adverse prognosis.

A few of the things that they made sure were present included relaxing music, loving photos, and paintings sent by my friends and their children. My family would also read lovely letters that were written to me. I still have a huge tote filled with all the loving cards that I received while recuperating. My family also made sure that I received physical affection, whether it was holding my hands, touching my arms, or hugging me. We have a common belief, that there are many occasions that touch can prove to be very therapeutic.

There is a plethora of science behind the effects of the energy surrounding you on your mental and physical health. We can allow ourselves the power of choice. We can decide whether or not to honk our horn, cut someone off while driving, be rude, make fun of someone, yell at anyone or be demanding. These are the things that we have all fallen victim to at one time or another. Sometimes we are the ones who show these responses, or we can also be the lucky recipient of such reactions. We all need to occasionally stop and take a few minutes for intentional breathing to calm down before we release this energy into the world.

We have to choose our battles, and we do have a choice. I am not saying, *"Oh, never get upset with anyone in any situation"*. I do NOT want to encourage anyone to hold on to their negative emotions. However, what I encourage is to consider how important the decision of choosing your battles can be. This way, the outcome for both parties can be optimized.

My family and friends were very present with me; they were loving, and they made sure to help me out in any way that they could. Neide, my friend who I introduced earlier as the ER doctor, was very supportive of my family and me. She would come to all of the group meetings with my family and my health care providers. She made us a priority in her life! She even spent her birthday at Craig Hospital at a meeting with us instead of celebrating in a more traditional way. She was an amazing resource for my family and me. The role she generously took was to be somewhat of a medical translator for the more detailed parts of my care. She would direct my family, asking the important questions that were imperative to understand.

Neide was in close contact with my doctors, helping me and my family in any way she could. She later shared with me that during the early stages, she was afraid that I would not survive the injuries. She spoke to the neurologist, and they shared a very grim outlook with her. Things did not look good! They said if I were to survive, they were not sure if I would be able to walk or talk, and they were pretty confident that I would not be able to take care of myself. Neide also told me that she was afraid that if I did make it, I would not like her anymore. This was not even a possibility in my mind, although they do say many people's personalities change after a brain injury.

Thankfully, we are both still very present in each other's lives. Let me share something interesting about our friendship. Neide, her family and I are on different ends of the political spectrum. Many times, we respectfully say to each other, *"I love you even though we have very different political beliefs!"* With this said, there are times when we can have an open political conversation and learn and expand our beliefs. This has taught me the lesson that it's important to be open and try to understand another person's perspective. Even though our beliefs range over a diverse spectrum, for me, it is a comforting feeling to have love and support from her and her family. We are human first, regardless of different opinions.

During this time in the hospital, I had many new experiences, pretty much daily! I have always been a very independent person, although things were extremely different at this challenging time in my life. Having to allow myself to accept help, I had to wear a very special back brace secondarily to my spine injury and had to move around using a wheelchair. Fortunately, I had a lot of support from my amazing team: Dr. Alan Weintraub, Dr. Alan Spees, Dr. Alvarez, Dr. Berry, and my great therapists Katie, Suzanne, and Michelle! They planned to stabilize me and my brain function before delving into the very invasive spinal surgery.

Being a pharmacist, I had a broad view of the role of physical, speech, and occupational therapists in healthcare; this experience further expanded my view. This incident opened my eyes and made me much more aware of the instrumental role the therapist plays as a member of the health care team. Their role in the recovery process of a patient is imperative.

All of my caregivers had their work cut out for them. Despite this trying time, I remained confident that I could make most people from my medical team laugh. This turned out to be especially true for Katie, my speech therapist. I recall that, at the beginning at Craig Hospital, I used to refer to people as massage or device, instead of their actual names. Later, finding humor in this word selection, I laughed, wondering if my brain knew I liked massages and devices, hence assigning new names to everyone.

The neuroplasticity of the brain fascinates me to no end! Through my experience, I've discovered that the brain can make huge shifts on a level that many cannot imagine. The brain can move from a very challenged state to having agreeable outcomes. In many ways, I feel this is how life is at times. One day you may feel like you are in a slump, and the next day you might have awe-inspiring connections and experiences. We have to be open to serendipity and gifts that may be right around the corner for us! My heart tells me that love, gratitude, positive energy, and a healthy environment had a fundamentally huge impact on my healing process. In life, there are no guarantees; let's try to optimize our days!

It is fascinating how therapeutic our surroundings can potentially be and the impact that they can have on the healing process. Studies reveal exciting findings regarding the impact of the architecture of a building on human health and healing. They show that a room with a view of the outdoors and nature in a hospital with increased amounts of natural light is associated with decreased perceived stress, reduced levels of pain, as well as a decreased use of analgesics.

My friend Charlie Schmidt is an architect. He is very conscious of optimizing the visual of the outside in his designs. This is because inviting in the beauty of the outdoors can facilitate a more positive experience in the building's interior. This is a very positive aspect of the world of architecture...allowing the light in.

My mom shared with me her perspective on this challenging time in my healing process. The words she shared with me are: *"Thank God you were coming back to life. Cyrina, you had to relearn the basic skills of life. It was as if you were passing through early childhood and adolescence all over again. You had to learn vocabulary, and you had to learn how to talk. Swallowing and walking were parts of the building blocks for the new life you wanted so badly. We celebrated every success, big or small. The rehabilitation was very demanding, but the team at Craig was extremely positive and skilled."*

The whole process was very interesting. Baby steps with encouragement from my family, therapist, and friends every step of the way was the process. My mother told me that watching me recover was like watching me grow up again: I was a child learning to walk, talk, and communicate again. Then, I started running, and they could not keep up with me! Thankfully, I am a resilient person and was able to lace up my running shoes and pick myself up to run to the most optimal outcome!

I was very excited about the progression of my healing path. In time, I was able to communicate somewhat effectively. Communication is such an important part of my life; although, I am not always a very effective communicator. I talk too much on many days and am confident that some people would rather that I become familiar with the practice of silence. Which, admittedly, is not my strong suit. Finally, when I was able to communicate with my family, my mother and I discussed life and how our journeys are always in flux and how there are no guarantees. At this time, I was still having trouble remembering words; and, at times, I would use the wrong word to describe my emotional state or the name of an object.

Even so, I took this chance to embrace and celebrate the fact that I was able to speak at all. I was conscious of the fact that I was definitely moving in the right direction! We, as humans, sometimes expect instant success or results; we beat ourselves up when we have not achieved the desired outcome right away. However, we have to try to keep optimism alive in our hearts and celebrate small victories and movement toward the desired outcome. This is a thought-provoking quote from happiness researcher Shawn Achor; I find that it closely parallels my life at that time: *"Small wins lead to momentum and allow your brain to actually achieve those large goals that you set for yourself."* Celebrating every victory, no matter how small, was a very important activity to adjust my mindset to overcome my challenges.

Humility was an emotion that I experienced on a very deep and tremendous level being a patient at Craig Hospital. Literally, I had someone by my side during all of my mobile waking hours. This meant zero privacy! Embarrassing as it was, I had someone in the bathroom with me at all times, even when I took a shower. One benefit was that I became more comfortable being naked in front of strangers; I really had no other option than to accept and embrace the process.

When a male medical assistant helped me shower, I would make a joke and say, "I took a shower with a man last night". (Not exactly the erotic shower I would like to have with a man)! This was my way of trying to make light of the situation and find a way to laugh. As things were, this was a heavy time, and it was not an easy process! Thank God I was mentally in a good place and could find humor even in such awkward circumstances.

The October before my accident, I was not in a good mental state. I felt very down and depressed at that time, which in itself was a very unusual experience for me. We undoubtedly all have hard days, but I had never had a solid month in my life when I felt weighed down by depressive feelings. My mental state alarmed me and motivated me to see my doctor. With all the new information about Vitamin D, I asked him if he would please test my Vitamin D level. We were both shocked by the results, my level was frighteningly low. This was strange since I spend a lot of time outdoors, and Colorado is one of the sunniest states. We know that being outdoors in the sun helps our bodies with the production of Vitamin D. We immediately started with supplements, and in about a month, thankfully I began feeling much better.

I would not have been able to handle such a traumatic event in my life if I was still dealing with depression. It's shocking how low my vitamin D levels were at that time. I decided to share this information with my family and friends, also encouraging them to have their levels tested. A few of them found out that they had low levels, as well. I am still not sure why there is such a high incidence of this deficiency.

As a pharmacist, I regularly recommended patients get their Vitamin D levels checked when they are being treated for depression. With my recommendation, a few of them had their levels tested; results showed many of them also had low Vitamin D levels. This test may be considered to ensure that there are no deficiencies that could lead to depression before or while taking antidepressants. Many times, we forget to look at the fundamental parts and rule out the potential of a more natural treatment by regaining balance within our bodies.

At times, there are limitations placed on activities in life which can prove to be very challenging. One limitation I had to deal with at this time was feeling very disconnected from my friends and my life. Talking is an area where I excel; and many times, I have the phone attached to my ear. I'm the friend who will always reach out and call even if I haven't talked to someone in years. As I mentioned earlier, for patients who have suffered a TBI, the medical professionals first try to minimize their stimulation. The same happened for me; being left without a phone because they felt that I needed limitations placed on me.

The first day that I was able to talk on the phone again was a glorious day in my life! I was certainly suffering from withdrawal; because, in general, I am pretty much addicted to my phone. My family had to monitor my use since I am officially a phone junkie. Once I had my phone back, I felt excited to talk with my friends and to feel connected with others again!

One of the most important calls I made was to Chris, an acquaintance who is a spine surgeon. I was suffering from a crushed T-7, which is located in the center of the spine and feeling terrified at the thought of undergoing spinal surgery. Without a doubt, if I sent my MRI to him, he would share with me his honest expert opinion. We have all heard those horror stories of patients who were told they needed surgery. But, in reality, they did not need to go through the challenging and risky procedure at all.

By reputation, surgeons like to cut. I wanted to make sure this surgery was necessary. Chris definitely had my best interest in mind. He was very supportive, and he confirmed my need for spine surgery. Though this was not what I was hoping to hear, it was a huge relief to have this resource in the form of a very caring and generous person who had taken the time to share his knowledge with me.

Support was all around me. Two of my best friends from Florida, Dawn, and Michelle (we have been friends since the eighth grade), flew out to see me. This was a huge gift of their time and a token of their sincerity and love for me because they both have families they had to leave at home. Dawn has four children, and Michelle has two. Their husbands were supportive and had made their trips to Colorado a possibility, which became a very welcomed reality for me!

Dawn and Michelle arrived before my back surgery was scheduled. Their visit was a good distraction for me since I was in quite a bit of pain due to my spine injury. The pain was constant, and it would shoot up and down my spine. There would, at times, be intermittent uncomfortable pressure in my lower back area. Any distraction from this pain was welcomed! I felt fortunate to have my friends offer their support and their love, which allowed me to be very vulnerable. Our trusted relationship allowed me to express my fears openly. Additionally, two sets of my cousins also flew out, while a few friends stopped by Craig Hospital to say hello and give me Big Hugs!

The number of people allowed to visit me at Craig Hospital was very limited because I couldn't be overstimulated. Marty and Ralph, a couple who were patients of mine at the pharmacy and dear friends, had come to visit me at Craig Hospital. I was so touched and thankful to have them in my life. Ralph still tells me that he prays for me all the time. I say to him: thank you, Ralph! I need all the prayers you can send my way.

The most important idea that I want to share with you is to celebrate the small things in life and to have gratitude. Life is all about love. My experience makes me want to encourage everyone to realize that they are not just a statistic. The world of Western medicine is very analytical, all about data and statistics. Yes, these are important; yet I feel that human connection must also be a priority when it comes to medicine. Not just the connections with others, the connection with yourself and your body is so important as well!

In the case of a not-so-positive prognosis, I want to encourage people to adopt the mindset that allows for multiple perspectives. I suggest this because, in life, multiple outcomes can occur. Regardless of your statistical prognosis, the outcome can be very different. After this experience, I have evolved into a person who reads more about the miracles and positive spontaneous healings that people experience in their lives; these have allowed me to learn essential life lessons from others' stories.

There are a large number of books available that illustrate this clearly. In *Proof of Heaven*, Eben Alexander MD, a neurosurgeon, wrote about his near-death experience. This was an extraordinary read and I highly recommend checking it out. Another amazing book is *Dying to Be Me* by Anita Moorjani, which is an unbelievable story about a woman's inspiring recovery. Both books illustrate that we should allow ourselves to believe in miracles, or outliers, or whatever word you like to use to describe off-the-charts, awe-inspiring healing journeys!

Anita's miraculous survival from cancer even inspired oncologists from America to fly over to Hong Kong with a desire to understand and learn more about her case and her unbelievable recovery. A few years after my accident, I had the opportunity to be present when both Anita Moorjani and Dr. Alexander spoke at my church at different times. I was able to meet Anita Moorjani afterward. She inspired me and has added another layer to my life, reaffirming my faith and understanding that there is more to existence than what is present on this earth. This is something that I also experienced with my accident. I saw how my world has expanded on multiple levels.

I became very familiar with several hospitals, though that was not exactly what had been on my agenda for the summer of 2010. Experiencing the pulse of the different hospitals was very interesting to me. The day came for me to transfer to another hospital for my back surgery. This was a layered journey for me. We will now shift and head to St. Anthony's Hospital for the long-awaited spine surgery. We will return to Craig Hospital in a few days because, though it may seem like it, my time at Craig was not yet over.

Takeaway Lessons from this Chapter:

※ Celebrate the baby steps! We, as Americans, tend to want everything done yesterday. Allow yourself to celebrate the journey and enjoy the moment.

※ The positive energy in your space is very important to facilitate more happiness and healing. I encourage us all to be conscious of our surroundings and set an intention to help foster positive elements in our world.

※ Try not to limit yourself. There are miracles; know and believe that things are not always black and white. Permit yourself to be the best you can be and generate a positive mentality that surrounds you.

※ Know that there is a time for everything while allowing yourself to be patient and continue to move on the path where you feel aligned and guided.

※ Be open and try to understand another person's perspective. Even though your beliefs may range over a diverse spectrum. We can learn and be open to different perspectives when we are constructive about our opinions.

※ If you feel psychologically less than optimal, you might want to have your Vitamin D levels tested.

※ The most conscious connection created in this chapter of my life was feeling a connection to my fellow patients at Craig Hospital. Knowing and seeing that there were others who were having major challenges on their journey also allowed me to know I was not alone!

※ What connections were created for you in Chapter 5?

Chapter 6

Spine Surgery

The significant days of our lives are often blueprinted in our minds. July 15, 2010, was one of those for me, as it was the day of my spinal surgery. Not surprisingly, this day required a ton of preparations. My sister, my advocate and my savior did an immense amount of research to bring the most capable surgeon possible for my surgery.

It is so fascinating how decisions we make today can impact our future, as we never know where things will lead. Recognizing this, I have always tried to live my life being open to the endless opportunities and possibilities that life offers. This is the way I want my life to unfold because this is how I can bring my most authentic self forward.

Dr. Brown, the spine surgeon who came to see me at Craig Hospital, is a wonderful person, as well as quite funny. He has been practicing for many years. At this time in his career, he would be assisting a young surgeon, whom he believed in, Dr. Henderhiser, who had just finished his fellowship. He was not even board certified when my sister chose him for this very important role that he would play in my world. He became certified the month of my surgery. Dr. Brown spoke very highly of Dr. Henderhiser. It is interesting because Dr. Brown had played an active role during the inception of Flight for Life®: part of the formula that saved my life!

The surgery could not be done at Craig Hospital, so I was transferred to St. Anthony's, where I met Dr. Henderhiser. He was a very nice young (only 33 at the time) man, who was also eye candy. Although I felt confident that I was in good hands, I was very nervous about having spine surgery. My family knew how I felt, and they were very supportive and encouraging throughout this difficult process. With this type of surgery, there is very little room, if any, for errors. Not having the surgery could have led me down the path to being paralyzed and I might never have been able to walk again. Not wanting this as a potential option, we opted to have surgery. I definitely needed all the love, support, prayers, and positive thoughts while going through this process that I had no control over. Having to surrender, as none of this was in my hands.

Diane, a family friend, who lives in Estes Park, Colorado, came down on several occasions to see us. Although I have no recollection of her many previous visitations, I do have a very clear memory of her visit during my time at St. Anthony's. She was very supportive of all of the Bullards during this challenging time! Diane lived in the town where I grew up. We attended the same Junior High and High School, so in 2010 we had known her for 20+ years. Diane is a talented artist whose work is very thoughtful, eclectic, and layered with meaning. She made an inspiring and extremely artistic gift that I want to share with you. Here is a photo of the gift that she created for me.

Included is the passage that Diane wrote to illustrate what she was thinking during her creative process.

"Malena called to let me know she was in Denver. I assumed she had just come for a getaway to visit you! Through tears, she explained your accident and asked if I might be able to come to the hospital. I told her I would be there the following morning. As I couldn't sleep, I went to my creative space and started looking at my things with a critical eye.

I wanted to create something that would give you, as well as the family, strength, and love. I wanted to capture your spirit and inner strength. It needed to be portable so that you could have it with you in the months ahead, no matter where you were. The Supergirl lunchbox was the perfect vessel. Because you hit your head, the crowns seemed obvious. There are three in the Spirit Box.

Healing light was a big theme, as well. I could only imagine you being closed inside of your body during that time, but your internal light was still shining. It would be the light that would grow as you healed. I felt that the canyon picture was your spirit, trying to break through the layers of your body and head that needed to heal.

The light is your fight. It also represents a higher power reaching out to connect to you. It is the energy of the universe surrounding you. The light bulbs around you represent your family. I wanted to include you, your Mom, Dad, Malena, Jason, and Justin. You Bullards are a pack and gain strength as a unit. The other stars and sequins represent all of your friends from around the world, so many, so vast, each praying for you. I wanted you to feel surrounded by their love.

You have a heart in your hand. It represents how freely you give YOUR love to those around you. The doll, of course, is you. High heels and a cute dress no matter what you are going through!" - Diane Collinet

Diane is another example of the amazing people I have been blessed with in my life, as well as the positive impact they have had on my healing process. The thought and details that Diane includes in her art is part of her talent; her use of stories is to celebrate and inspire. This beautiful piece is in my bedroom on a special shelf, so I see the Super Girl vessel symbolic art every day. It always brings a smile to my face whenever I look at this meaningful and thoughtful gift!

Right before my surgery, all the doctors came by to share the time frame of the surgery and what to expect. The surgery took a little over eight hours. Thankfully, I came out on the other side, after being sedated for so long. I felt completely out of it for quite some time after the surgery. I was super relieved to come out of the surgery alive! However, I felt drugged up and out of it, and it took some time for me to register where I was and what was going on. After a spinal fusion, my body was hooked up to many monitors. Being watched very closely to make sure that all was moving in the right direction.

Finally transferred back to my room, I continued the much-needed pain medication. The pain that I experienced after the surgery was intense.

Since I have never birthed a child or experienced anything else of that physical magnitude of pain, I can say that this was a new experience for me. I felt somewhat surprised at the elevated level of suffering since my threshold for pain is relatively high. I am definitely not a whiner! Having had a spinal fusion, I am now a proud owner of titanium rods and screws from T-4 to T-10, the thoracic region of the spine.

My mom remembers this time very well. She was my rock, and this is what she had to say about this part of the challenging and layered journey: *"The condition of her brain was becoming better but her fracture of T7 needed to be addressed. Researching an orthopedic surgeon with proper skills put her sister on the frontline. The decision was made with much consideration of details. Cyrina was transferred to St. Anthony's, and the family gathered around her for support.*

After about eight and a half hours of surgery, we went to see her in recovery. Her body was swollen, and her skin had turned a shade of green. She had received eight units of blood and was in extreme pain. I felt like we had taken so many steps backward.

Her first night was so very difficult. Thank God the emergency department physician knew Cyrina. Dr. Garyfallou was dating Kerri, one of Cyrina's friends. He was very nice and came to check in on her. He was a lifeline and facilitated a follow-up for her and made sure that her pain was controlled, and she was more comfortable."

Luckily, the heavy-duty drugs helped to keep my pain at a tolerable level. Knowing there would be a lot of healing and physical therapy in my future, pain medications were going to become a staple in my diet. While I realized what a mysterious process life could be, I had to put on my seat belt to be ready for this part of the ride. I began by taking baby steps, all the while making sure that I celebrated the small victories on my path. This was the key that helped me with my mindset. It gave me the confidence to move through this while believing that everything would be alright. This was my reality and what I was experiencing. This is life, and I have to know I will make it through the battles that are presented to me. This situation was truly a battle. I do not wish this experience on anyone.

My scheduled time at St. Anthony's was five days; however, my bowels decided to make other plans. This meant they were not moving, nor was I. Here is a slightly embarrassing, and what many would probably call TMI, part of this painful process. With all the much-needed painkillers, I became unbelievably constipated. They could not discharge me until I had a bowel movement. Oh, the rules! Here we go! I am being very vulnerable and authentic, sharing this unpleasant part of my journey.

Already in tremendous torment from my back surgery, constipation added a whole extra level of pain. Now I had the pleasure of being given an enema. My situation was magnified, and the story evolved to an extreme level on the humiliating rating scale.

The on-duty nurse, who had the unpleasant job of administering the enema, of course, was male. He was also very nice, extremely attractive, and straight. Wow! I was about to be part of a formula that does not occur all that often. In disbelief, I thought to myself: "Really? Is this actually happening? A hot, straight male nurse, who happens to be nice, will be giving me an enema?" Yes, I was the lucky one who got to check this experience off my bucket list.

However, the pain was intense, and the tears rolled down my face. The bedpan was the collection device we had to use. It was neither the most comfortable nor the most attractive way to evacuate anyone's bowels.

It was a very long and painful process, but finally...victory! As a pharmacist, I knew that constipation was a potential and common side effect of narcotics. However, this experience in my life made me realize how important it is to have regular bowel movements, especially while on pain medications. I guess humility was the lesson I needed to learn as I was getting an overdose of humiliating experiences.

As a result, this experience shifted how I counseled patients on the use of narcotic pain medication going forward. Since then, I have made sure patients knew how vital it is to have their bowels in motion while on these medications. After this experience, I have gained such gratitude for normal, non-painful, bowel movements. This event definitely has helped me move through the many challenges that I faced during this time.

With cleared bowels and successful spine surgery, my heart felt lighter! I was excited to be alive and to be able to move all my extremities (and my bowels)! In my mind, Dr. Henderhiser is an outlier because not only is he a very talented surgeon, but he is also a humble and nice human being. Dr. Henderhiser, who has obviously played a huge role in my life, and his wife are now friends of mine. Both are such incredible people who bring a positive light to our world!

My time at St. Anthony's was relatively short, but it was packed with intensity. On the 6th day, it was time for me to say goodbye to St. Anthony's and travel back to Craig Hospital.

Takeaway Lessons from this Chapter:

❋ Many days we as humans take so much for granted. It is truly a gift to be able to walk, talk, or even feed ourselves. These gifts can be taken away at any time. Having gratitude is something that can help all of us travel through the challenging times in life, knowing and believing that we will be okay.

❋ Celebrating on the way to our goals helps to bring them to fruition. The average person cannot say that they are going to run a marathon; training is required to attain the goal. Celebrate little victories and feel happy for every mile that you gain. Then, you can extrapolate from your smaller victories; you can expand and achieve the larger goals that you have in life. This is how you enjoy the journey.

❋ Having nourishing relationships is yet another aspect of life that is very important. We never know why someone is placed in our path. Kindness, connection, care, community, and communication can help us cultivate a relationship that, in 20 years, may become an important source of friendship, support, and love. I am encouraging everyone to be nice because of the positive energy that flows from this good; it fills not only your world but the world of others.

❋ The most conscious connection created in this chapter of my life was feeling connected to Diane. The gift of her artwork was an illustration of how well she knew me and my family and the incredible support she was able to share with our family.

❋ What connections were created for you in Chapter 6?

Chapter 7

Back to Craig

Finally, armed with the all-important back brace, having had a successful surgery and bowel movement, I was ready to be transported back to Craig Hospital. Although returning to a familiar place, my summer home of 2010, it was not exactly for a summer vacation. It was time for me to continue my intense and challenging rehabilitation. A multitude of areas had to be addressed after suffering such extreme types of injuries, not just in my physical body but also in the psychological realm.

Psychological rehabilitation was a much-needed part of the formula, secondary to the limitations that I was experiencing after having spinal surgery. At this point in my recovery, I was introduced to yet another extremely humbling situation. I guess I needed to learn a huge lesson of humility, and it was granted to me in larger quantities than I had ever imagined possible.

After surgery, my range of motion was limited, and my movement was restricted. If having someone in the bathroom with you at all times is not challenging enough, let us up that humbling factor 10 notches. Now, I not only needed to have someone in the bathroom with me while having a bowel movement, I had to accept someone's help to wipe my ass.

Never in my life had I thought of being in this situation! This was one of the hardest things for me to accept. I am sure anyone will agree with me when I say this is not the most flattering activity. Let's just say life can be an interesting roller coaster. This essential ability to wipe one's ass is an activity that most of us take for granted. When I had to surrender and accept help, it was one of the most challenging moments in my life.

The medical assistants acted like this was no big deal, which was reassuring and comforting. They knew I was dealing with elevated levels of humiliation. Despite my many different levels of embarrassment, there really were no other options for me. As a result, it made me have a whole new appreciation for many things. It specifically magnified the need to not take the seemingly little things in life for granted. Luckily, everyone was very kind, and they all tried to help me feel normal. Although during this time, I never really felt that way.

It felt miraculous that I was walking with a walker only a few days after my surgery. The positive impact that modern medicine has in our lives is truly amazing. Thanks to a skilled spine surgeon, I was doing incredibly well. With intense PT, I continued to improve my ability to walk. However, it was a process. Walking is yet another activity many of us take for granted.

I was on major pain killers and had to make sure I got a dose every four hours, or the pain became too extreme. It is interesting because I had numbness as well as pain in my back at the same time. My back suffered from pressure and nerve pain, and there were certain areas I could not even feel. It is apparently normal to have numbness secondary to all the nerves that were affected during the surgery. The pain medication was absolutely necessary every day for about four months. Thankfully, I do not have an addictive personality, at least to drugs. I was able to wean off the medication successfully. As a pharmacist, I have witnessed many people who were not successful in discontinuing their pain medications. Sadly, these drugs can lead people to very dark places. Currently, I have had to restart taking the pain medication. I will share my reasoning for this decision with you later in our journey.

Physical therapy was a daily activity to help me improve my balance, so I could start walking again. With the help and guidance of my physical therapist, Katie, I had graduated from a wheelchair to a walker, and now was going to start physical therapy to be able to walk on my own. Learning how to walk again definitely had its challenges. I am a runner. Not a fast one, but I have run many 5 K's, 10 K's, half-marathons as well as one full marathon of 26.2 miles.

Surprised to discover that walking for only about 30 feet made me feel so exhausted, I had to sit down for a few minutes. I was shocked! I felt so defeated! This experience reinforced for me the saying, "If you do not use it, you will lose it." To be able to walk efficiently with stability and not become exhausted immediately seemed like a dream to me. That day it became clear my rehabilitation was going to be a difficult and long journey. I forced myself to focus on it as my mission.

After that day, I experienced an overwhelming feeling of defeat. Again, I had to remind myself to celebrate the small victories. I kept telling myself repeatedly, "Hey, lady, you may tire quickly, but you are walking!"

We have to remind each other not to beat ourselves up. In life, many things are easier in theory. It is easy to say, but it is challenging to practice it. I discovered I have to check in with myself every once in a while to take inventory of the positive things in my life.

Having a conversation, sitting up, increasing my range of motion, remembering words, and other little steps along the way became regular celebrations. This was part of my journey, and I was going to soar! This couldn't have happened if I had allowed myself to feel sorry for my situation. Although, sometimes I did fall down that path. Then, I'd remind myself to have patience and to know there was progression in the right direction. Best of all, there were many cheerleaders in my corner, and I am thankful for all of them!

CaringBridge® website was such an inspiring and incredible gift. When I was able to read the entries and all of the loving messages for me, it gave me more confidence and a greater sense of purpose. I was surprised and touched by what some people had written. Before reading the messages, I didn't know I meant that much to so many individuals. It was only after going through this situation that I discovered how many people truly cared about me. What a gift to unfold for me during this challenging time in my life!

Starting to feel stable on my feet, I was walking better. I was now able to walk outside with a medical assistant. It was very exciting! Craig Hospital has such great resources for its patients. The Therapeutic Recreation Center, also known as T-REC, is a department that provides activities so patients can have fun, play games, and laugh. These activities were essential for us, the patients. We needed a break from our intense reality and an opportunity to feel good and have fun!

One of my most memorable experiences at Craig Hospital was the 'Hobie Cat Day,' an awesome event! They transported the patients (many were paralyzed and in wheelchairs) to the Cherry Creek Reservoir. There awaited a vast BBQ, a band, and many social activities, with multiple Hobie Cats, so that we could have an adventurous day! For each patient on a boat, there was a person who was responsible for making sure we were safe. No falling off the boat and no drowning allowed!

It was a beautiful Colorado day. Even though I was wearing a back brace, I felt like a human being with no limitations. That was so empowering! Being on the water gave me hope and confidence that I was going to be okay. I was able to enjoy my time by sailing, laughing, having fun, and enjoying the music and the company that day. As my Mom was able to join me, it was such a memorable day for her as well. The experiences of that day were very encouraging and inspiring!

Another significant event was when I was able to go on a field trip with my family. I was granted a leave for dinner one night, my mom, sister, my brother, Jason, and I went to dinner together. They told me to choose whichever restaurant I wanted and Sushi Den it was! I love this restaurant; enjoying the evening was a wonderful experience. It was a "normal night out" with my family and one where we had fantastic food.

Thinking back to this time, it probably was one of the nicest restaurants my family, as a group, had ever dined. Although we had a lot of fun that night, we really missed my other brother Justin, and his partner Tim. We were the family that was used to going to Denny's for dinner, especially on birthdays, because it meant a free meal. In contrast, Sushi Den is a place that draws in tourists and travelers when they are visiting Denver. Moreover, I was excited to spend time there and share this experience with my family. This evening out was part of the baby steps taken to begin my journey back into the community.

Every experience helped me grow and return to my pre-accident life, even though many things were different now. One of the projects my occupational therapist, Michelle, wanted me to accomplish was hosting my own dinner party at the hospital for six guests, who were fellow patients. Michelle had me create the menu. Then she took me to the grocery store to buy all the ingredients for dinner. I set the table, prepared the meal, and greeted my guests. It was a fun and rewarding activity for me to put everything together for this dinner party. I felt very accomplished because entertaining is one activity that I love.

My therapist told me to prioritize doing the things that I loved. I was able to prepare a good meal and entertain my guests successfully. Everyone enjoyed my culinary creations, or at least they said they did. That was another very affirming event that reassured me that things were going to be okay.

Although progressing rapidly in the right direction, I still had memory challenges. One rule was established with my family and friends: if I had trouble remembering a word, they were not to tell it to me. Challenging my brain was necessary so I put my frontal lobe to work! Sometimes, when having a tough time with certain words, I would ask them to tell me the first letter of the word. I still had to think about what the word was, but I did not want to be spoon-fed. This was a gradual process. It was strenuous and frustrating for me some days. And other days it went smoothly. I share this insight with many people, even strangers. It was a team effort moving through this part of the healing process.

My speech therapist was very encouraging. I had to learn to speak again and, hopefully, in a way that made sense. I found myself speaking a little slower than usual, as I was thinking and processing as I spoke. At least I was not calling everyone 'massage' or 'device' anymore. My mother reminded me again, *"You were learning how to talk and walk. Then you started running, and we were not able to keep up with you!"* There was no doubt in my mind that I was going to win this battle and be more than okay. There's a quote from Buddha I wholeheartedly believe in: *"What we think, we become."*

This time in my life allowed me to have the experience of building relationships with my fellow patients. I became connected to many of them. They understood the obstacles I was dealing with and how this felt. People face such a range of challenges in our world; and at Craig Hospital, these situations were magnified. The patients at this hospital fought a huge spectrum of injuries. We all had our individual battles.

Another memory I will never forget came during lunch one day in the cafeteria with a fellow patient named Mark. We shared our stories, and we connected, although I was taken aback by his story. His wife Robyn and he were riding on a motorcycle having a great day when things suddenly shifted for them. A serious motorcycle accident caused Mark to suffer a TBI and a spinal cord injury. What followed in his story really touched my heart. When they had the accident, his wife was pregnant. She had suffered minor injuries, but thankfully, she had not lost the baby.

I cannot imagine the worry this accident must have caused them both on so many levels. I kept Mark and Robyn in my prayers, imploring that all would be okay with their unborn child. We are still in contact today, and I am happy to report they did have a happy and healthy little boy. They now have two beautiful children, an adorable little boy and girl. If you would like to know more about their story, please read their book: *58 Feet: The Second That Changed Our Lives*, by Mark and Robyn Glaser.

I had many sincere and very heartfelt conversations when I was at Craig Hospital; because when someone almost dies, they become much more real and connected with love. Many of the patients at Craig Hospital had had similar experiences, situations, fears, and challenges. This allowed us to be real, not superficial. Since most of us could have died, being shallow really did not serve us now. In general, I have been real and authentic my entire life. I have never, well, almost never, been a gossiper. When people want to have me share dirt or drama, in general, I say to them, "We are experiencing a challenging situation, I wish them the best". Truth be told, there have been a handful of times when I have not been so tactful!

Near the end of my stay at Craig Hospital, two of my dear friends were getting married. The hospital allowed my sister to take me to their wedding, which turned out to be another amazing field trip. It was a beautiful day, and the venue was great. The bride, Kim, looked amazing and her hubby-to-be, Steve, looked very handsome! I was so thankful to be able to celebrate Kim and Steve's wedding day. As we have so many mutual friends, it was wonderful to see everyone again.

I was able to wear a lovely dress; it was accented with an ever-so-stylish back brace that day, so you can say I was going for the nontraditional fashion plate award! I do believe I created the back- brace style that day. It was all relative. I was walking and talking, and this made me thankful to be sporting the back brace. My sister was so loving, supportive, and extremely helpful as she made this adventure possible for me!

Troy and Kat, mutual friends of Kim, Steve and me, were at the wedding. For many years, Troy and Kat have lived in Vail, where Troy owns a ski and bike shop located in Vail Village. They are extremely outdoorsy people who know how to have fun! As they are very connected to the mountain community, Troy was able to get my bike from the police. He is a very bike-savvy guy, and he completely repaired my bike. I was so thankful for his efforts and the time that he spent to be so thoughtful and caring towards me. Although I was unable to accept his generous gift because I did not ever want to ride that bike again. Just the same, I was incredibly touched and thankful for his generosity and time.

While I shared my thanks for his time and thoughtfulness, I wanted him to sell the bike or do whatever he wanted to with the bike. This act added to the bucket of reasons that I felt so supported on my journey. People are wonderful! The beautiful wedding was a grand celebration of the lovely couple and their amazing family and friends. This storybook wedding at a fantastic venue gave me time to reconnect with dear friends.

The hospital was excellent at addressing all the physical and psychological aspects of health care, and most of each patient's needs. But the spiritual domain, I felt, was not supported. Realizing that not everyone is open to the spiritual realm, I still believe that all domains: the physical, the spiritual, the mental, and the emotional, should be addressed and supported. So much information is available about the importance of each of these areas of our lives. Notably, if one area is drained, the other areas will suffer. It is the emotional domain that is most commonly drained.

For example, if you feel emotionally drained, will you want to work out and use your physical domain? I feel strongly that we must treat the whole person and encourage everyone to be centered in their lives. Since we are all wired differently, it helps to facilitate healing when you get to know a person and understand what holds importance to them, personally and environmentally. I reference and credit HeartMath® for sharing with me this fascinating information about the different domains.

As a certified trainer and coach for HeartMath®, I learned this information and the science behind the intelligence of the heart.

Hospitals have to be conscious of the cost of care. As a result, they are limited in what they can provide. My experience has made me wonder if volunteers could facilitate bringing these important elements into the patient's world. Maybe they can do that with music by making sure a Pandora® or Spotify® station is playing the patient's favorite type of music. Or if the patient likes to play games, a volunteer could go to the room and spend time engaging that patient. If we were able to see what the patient loves and what brings happiness to them, this could be valuable information. We may be able to incorporate a few activities to support what they love and treat the whole person.

Even watching a funny movie, or a comedian who the patient likes, brings some positive vibes to their day. I suggest this because we know laughter plays a huge part in bringing positivity to the energy in our world!

A quote from Earl Nightingale: *"Learn to enjoy every minute of your life. Be happy now. Don't wait for something outside of yourself to make you happy in the future. Think how really precious the time you have to spend, whether it's at work or with your family. Every minute should be enjoyed and savored."*

This quote really resonated with my heart. His words always make me want to optimize this gift called life! When I was a patient at Craig Hospital, I was dealing with a lot. Often, happiness was not a concern, since surviving was the focus. With that said, Craig Hospital was great at introducing fun activities, which granted us laughter, creativity, and a sense of community. Our day was not all medical treatments and therapy. They incorporated many activities to facilitate fun. I needed to take the inspiring attitude from Earl Nightingale away with me, as I prepared for the journey back to my home.

Takeaway Lessons from this Chapter:

❋ Realize the gift of being able to take care of yourself and have gratitude for this gift! So often, we take this for granted, without understanding that this is a gift that can be taken away from us at any time.

❋ Happiness is something we can decide to incorporate into our day. It is our decision. Embrace it!

❋ Allow yourself to introduce activities in your day that facilitate happiness: music, dance, laughter, comedy, or whatever brings you happiness.

❋ Keep your physical, mental, spiritual, and emotional tanks full. Spiritual, in my mind, is not the same as religion. To me, spiritual means feeling connected, whether that is to God, a higher power, yourself, nature, or another person. In my mind, it is all the times that you feel fully present, aligned, and connected.

❋ True and authentic honesty is key. You do not need to have a serious accident to have heartfelt conversations. Try not to get caught up in the *things* of the world (cars, homes, boats, fancy clothing, shoes, et cetera). Value the quality of people and make real connections filled with love.

❋ The most conscious connection created in this chapter of my life was feeling connected to my family. They were helping every step of the way and supported me as we were taking baby steps to reintegrate myself into the world and my life.

❋ What connections were created for you in Chapter 7?

Chapter 8

Discharged Home

At long last, my discharge day from Craig Hospital arrived; I was finally leaving my summer home of 2010. That year I spent two and a half months in hospitals. Now, I could feel my home calling my name. Excited for my discharge, however, I knew I would miss all of the people I had become so close with during my summer stay.

My occupational therapist, Michelle, visited my home before I was discharged to help my family make my space as safe as possible. Since I was still experiencing secondary balance challenges, they were trying to decrease the number of obstacles I would face, developing a safe and optimal experience with everyday activities. For example, there were handlebars installed in the bathroom near the shower and toilet. They needed to optimize my environment to help foster success in my recovery.

My family was tremendously supportive, thorough and helpful through the challenges I faced during the summer of 2010. They were there every step of the way. And with each transition, they helped to make it as smooth as possible. This meant making my house safe for the disabilities I was experiencing. While showering, I still had to sit on a chair; also, my sister was always to be with me. I was going through some definite nontraditional experiences during this process.

I do remember very vividly the first day I took a shower by myself. After a very long time, I was able to stand in the shower without needing to use a chair. Wow, I felt so victorious! Very happily I celebrated this win, which was a huge step for me! This provided yet another illustration of how much of our daily living we take for granted. That moment of triumph and accomplishment, when I was able to stand alone in the shower, showed me that I would feel grateful during many moments in my future life. Gratitude and I became very in sync at this time in my life, and gratitude has remained a huge focus of mine every day since!

I felt very excited to be back home and in my beautiful neighborhood! I lived a few blocks away from a popular street in the Highlands area in Denver. This area has a lot of local shops, restaurants, and boutiques. Being an older part of Denver, it has great character. The neighborhood is friendly to walkers and has access to public transportation everywhere. It has plenty of resources when someone is unable to drive.

My sister and I used to walk to 32nd Ave and go to lunch or dinner just to get out of the house. I remember, walking arm in arm one day with my sister when I tripped, and she caught and stabilized me. This incident made me very conscious of the uneven sidewalks and their potential to cause accidents. My sister was hyper-vigilant. Lovingly, she pointed out the potential hazards I needed to be conscious of in different areas for this period in my life.

Being back in my home fostered many feelings as I was slowly regaining my life. Yet, I was still extremely tired and shocked at how much sleep my body needed. With that said, sleep is a huge part of the healing process, although I felt somewhat unproductive. In the end, I had to embrace and welcome my sleep. Luckily, I had devoted people helping me to keep my awake hours occupied.

Of my many wonderful friends who came to visit me at home, a few stand out in my mind. Like my friend Jeremy, who is creative and thinks outside the box. The medical professionals encourage patients, after a TBI, not to drink alcohol for at least one year after the injury. Even though I am not a heavy drinker, I enjoy a nice glass of red wine. Furthermore, I live in a state which is the home of popular artisanal brewpubs with super tasty and creative beers. Knowing these facts, my thoughtful friend Jeremy came over with a four-pack of an excellent Root Beer. His imaginative and thoughtful gift deeply touched my heart.

Now I would like to introduce you to my "gay husband," Rob, who is such an important person in my world. Rob and I had met in pharmacy school. While we were friendly in school, I would say we were only acquaintances who hung out with each other casually. Later in life, we reconnected in Orlando and had a blast after I moved back to Florida in 2000.

I moved back to Florida because friends asked me to watch their home and my old boss called and said he had a position for me. House - sitting for my friends, who owned an exquisite beachfront home, offered me many great opportunities. During this time, my friend Rob would come to visit, and this started the growth of our extraordinary friendship. We motivated each other and competed in many sprints and Olympic distance triathlons. Together, we had so much fun, as we traveled all around Florida to do these races. One day when we were training on the beach, he asked me, *"What will you do when the house-sitting gig is over?"* I said, "I do not know." Then he asked, *"Would you like to be my Grace?"* I was so touched! I accepted his offer to live together and for him to be my "Will."

This started a great journey in our friendship; we were incredible roommates for three years.

We had a blast together, as our home was filled with fun, laughter, and great times! We were both Pharmacists for Publix; therefore, we were colleagues, housemates, and friends. Many nights we motivated each other to exercise after working a 12-hour shift. Since we were colleagues, we would share our stories from the day and give each other feedback on how to deal with certain situations while on our run.

One day Rob asked me, *"Why do you think we are such good housemates?"* My explanation was: "Because we have no sexual tension." He is an attractive guy, although his characteristics are too effeminate for my taste. Our friendship has grown over the years, and I feel he is part of my family. During my recovery, Rob came to visit multiple times, as he is extremely loving and a very supportive friend. Today, Rob and his husband, David, continue to be important people in my life. I'm still Rob's Grace, and he is my Will.

Another memorable visit was from my great friend Eric Moose, "Moose" to his friends. Moose is a firefighter friend of mine from Florida. His visit occurred when my sister had to leave for California and she did not want me to be alone. Moose came to stay while she was gone. When Malena flew out, she left my car with a hidden key at the airport, so that Moose was able to drive my car to my home. After a TBI, no-one is allowed to drive until medically cleared, and they have to retake the written and driving test at the DMV.

Moose was a rock star who came out for ten days and was my handyman and chauffeur. He met many of my friends in Denver. An extreme handyman, Moose was able to do tons of projects and help with many of the things that needed to be fixed. I was so thankful to him for his support and love during this challenging time in my life. We are still very good friends, continuing to be in each other's lives since 2001.

One night when Moose was here, we walked to a local restaurant for dinner, where I ran into a friend of mine, Niya. When I told her about my summer of 2010, Niya said, *"Oh you should see my mom."* I thought about it, and remembering that Niya and I used to take dance classes from her mother, I said, "I do not think I will be signing up for dance classes now." She laughed and said, *"No, she is also a massage therapist."* I had no idea!

Later, I contacted Ahva, her mom. Ahva was such a gift that I call her my little angel. She is a very generous soul! She came to pick me up and drive me to her studio, where she gave me a massage; and then drove me home. I felt so thankful to her for her kindness in my life! I continue to be friends with many members of Ahva's family. I have been so thankful that I ran into Niya that day since that interaction has brought such light and help into my world.

The next big adventure was my first post-accident plane ride to Marisa and Brian's wedding in Austin, Texas. I was so excited to celebrate my friends' wedding on 10/10/10. (I love that date!) Neide, Kerri, and I flew together to Austin, and they were so gracious, lifting my heavy luggage and helping me in any way they could. We had such a nice celebration with our friends and their families.

The wedding was beautiful, and I was so thankful to be there. Marisa has such a loving and fun family! I am also impressed with her husband, Brian, a go-getter, and incredibly accomplished man, who is responsible and successful! I feel very happy for my friend that she has found a man who is a match for her. I am sure they will build a great life together. The reception was in Austin, in an extremely beautiful old hotel, The Driskill. We had a great time celebrating Marisa and Brian!

The first time I was at the airport, I was under the assumption that I would set off the alarms at the security check because of the hardware in my back. I was pleasantly surprised to discover that this did not happen. When I asked Dr. Henderhiser, my orthopedic surgeon, he informed me that I was now wired with titanium, which does not trigger the alarms. I was so excited to know this! I love to travel, and I did not want the TSA line to become a time-consuming obstacle in my life.

Even though I was traveling with friends to Austin, I felt a sense of independence. My first flight was an important step in my healing process. This event taught me the importance of being vulnerable and allowing myself to ask for help. I believe we all need to allow giving and receiving in our world. Hopefully, we all have a phase in our lives when that lightbulb goes off for us. There are times in life that we grow and learn exponentially. I have always been a giver, not a receiver. Recently, though, I have allowed myself to become more balanced in this realm. In most situations, I have begun to allow my needs to be met before I help others with theirs. This has led to a significant lesson in my life. When we are depleted and not taking care of ourselves, we are unable to bring our best self forward for our friends, our loved ones, or even for ourselves.

It was time for my family to become reacquainted with their own lives and reintegrate into their worlds. They had spent over five months with me, making sure I had all the necessary resources, love, and encouragement I needed, and that I would be fine in their absence. It was hard to say goodbye, even though I knew I must start living my own life, and they needed to return to theirs. Thankfully, I have many amazing friends who were happy and willing to help out; however, I had to learn to be more comfortable asking them for help. I became quite conscious about receiving help and expressing gratitude for the amazing, serendipitous events that were occurring. I even had a few more friends who were coming out to visit, and I was excited to have their company.

At this time, I was walking a lot. Definitely in a groove, I was taking the bus by myself to Craig Hospital at least three times a week for therapy! My rehabilitation was a thorough and demanding process. I became quite savvy with the public transportation system. Before my mom left, we had ridden the bus together. She came with me because she wanted to make sure I would be okay. My mother is probably one of the most loving and wonderful people in our world, as she lives from her heart! She is full of love; although she, like all of us, is not without fault. Yes, I am a little partial because she is my mom. However, if you were to ask anyone who knows her, without a doubt, 99% of them would say the same. She is truly a blessing!

The public transportation became my primary mode of travel all over Denver, most often to Craig Hospital. Riding the bus was a very educational and eye-opening experience! You never knew who you might meet and what interesting conversations could evolve.

I remember one time when the bus came to a stop and was picking up a person in a wheelchair. Many thoughts rushed through my mind as I reflected upon when I was in a wheelchair, waiting for my back surgery. I could have been that person. This was another reminder for me to try and be in the moment and to have gratitude for all that I have been given. The fact was that I could walk!

Years later, a few girlfriends and I were sitting around a fire pit in a beautiful back yard. We had glasses of wine and each other's company. Although everyone there was an independent professional woman, we were all participating in a bitchfest about how none of us had boyfriends. All of a sudden, a wave of reality hit me. I decided to share it with my friends, saying, "Let's stop our bitchfest and be thankful! We do not live in war-torn Syria, and we all have a great glass of wine in our hands, in a beautiful backyard with great friends." I knew gratitude was what we should have had in our hearts.

Let's get back to Craig Hospital and the physical, occupational, and speech therapy outpatient services that I attended for three days a week. As I have said, my rehabilitation was a very thorough process. I was assigned to all-new outpatient therapists, Celeste, Michelle, and Suzanne, who helped me become more functional and independent. It was their help that let me ease back into my independent life, which I had been longing to regain. Two other major activities at Craig Hospital were learning to drive again and working in their pharmacy. I will delve into my driving experience later in my story.

Being a pharmacist and having the diagnosis of a TBI is not exactly a favorable formula. I had the opportunity to work as an Intern at the Craig Hospital Inpatient Pharmacy. The pharmacists were very encouraging, intelligent, and motivating. I played different roles: order entry, filling prescriptions, and medication accuracy check. It is the responsibility of the pharmacist to always double-check the intern's work. This process impacted my healing because it fostered my confidence in my professional career. At Craig Hospital, I was able to have intellectual conversations with the pharmacists and to successfully perform all of the actual job requirements. With these accomplishments, my confidence was growing daily. I believe this was the key to my positive transition back to my profession. Tiffany, the community reintegration specialist at Craig Hospital was so helpful throughout this process of returning to employment.

The fact I was able to have the experience of working in the pharmacy was a pivotal event in my life. I felt uneasy and very self-conscious before I started interning at the Craig Hospital Pharmacy. Working as a Pharmacist again, I felt such a sense of relief to have had that internship experience. Thankfully, now I was able to function with my colleagues on a professional level.

All of my outpatient therapists played instrumental roles in my re-entering into the new normal and being able to function at my optimal level! Because it was a rigorous process, I am so thankful that Craig Hospital did not discharge me and say "goodbye and good luck."

The team at Craig Hospital held my hand and helped me to regain the skills necessary for a successful transition and reintegration into my life. I continued with outpatient services for about three and a half months after my discharge. My personal life was moving in a very positive direction. The path I was on was beginning to feel a little smoother and brighter. A big celebration in my life was occurring during the beginning of my outpatient therapy. The time had come for me to shift into the next decade of my life! Join me as we travel to the celebration next.

Takeaway Lessons from this Chapter:

❋ Giving and accepting help from others is a very important key to life.

❋ Obstacles sometimes come with gifts. Being conscious of how we view things in our life is important.

❋ Gratitude is a key to happiness.

❋ Root beer is a good and fun substitute for alcohol when needed!

❋ A "Will and Grace" friendship can be a benefit to your life.

❋ The most conscious connection created in this chapter of my life was feeling connected to my home and neighborhood. Having a sense of peace being back at home and knowing I was moving forward toward regaining my life.

❋ What connections were created for you in Chapter 8?

Chapter 9

The 5th Decade

Another significant day of my life is September 12, 2010. On this day I was gifted with celebrating another birthday! There had been a time, however, when the doctors were not sure if I would even live past 39 years. Through the grace of God and the loving, gifted, and dedicated individuals in my life, I had defeated all odds to celebrate my 40th birthday. Hopefully, you can understand why this day had such significance in my world. Having been through enough to know the value of my life now, I had no doubt about celebrating and honoring my existence.

My birthday celebration gave me a chance to see friends whom I had not seen in quite some time! A semi-funny coincidence about this day is an ongoing joke between my mother and me. Luckily, in my younger years, I had been blessed with 20/20 vision. My mother has always teased me by saying, *"Wait until you turn 40, Cyrina; that will change!"* Now I tease her and say, "Mom, I not only turned 40, but I also have had a traumatic brain injury!" With my accident, I suffered damage to my optic nerve. Now nearsighted, the opposite of what usually occurs around age 40. Today, I am the proud owner of glasses that are much-needed for driving. Without them, those darn signs on the road are very blurry, and I become a danger to everyone else traveling along the same highway.

Back to the birthday celebration. Jen, General Manager of Lola, a fantastic local restaurant, was able to reserve BeLola, the downstairs area of this local hot spot. The thought that so many of my friends and family had come was very overwhelming and heartwarming. I was happy, honored, and so thankful for being given this celebration. I intended to have a meaningful connection with everyone that night. Since many of my friends had chosen to be there, I knew it was going to be impossible for me to spend a lot of time with any one person. However, I was able to get many big hugs, and we did share lots of laughter. This night bestowed another strong life memory for me to cherish.

My mom, my sister Malena, and my brother Jason had come to celebrate; however, my other brother Justin and his partner Tim were unable to join us. They were in Cologne, Germany, where Justin was competing in the Gay Games. These international competitions had their inception in 1982 and were initially known as the Gay Olympics. I am going to pause with my story and shift gears for a bit because I want to share a little about my brother. I am very proud of Justin and his accomplishments! A determined hard worker, he had won a bronze medal in swimming at the Gay Games. I think it is interesting that I had never even heard of the Gay Games until he had participated in them.

But more than that, Justin and Tim got married in 2015 on their 19th anniversary! I credit them with having the most successful relationship in our family. Growing up Roman Catholic during the 70s and 80s meant that most of our community did not embrace homosexuality. My siblings and I had gone to Catholic school, where homosexuality was considered a sin. Moreover, both of my brothers had been altar boys for years in the Catholic Church. My mother is a Eucharistic minister. She is the only one who still practices Catholicism, the religion that has played a significant role in all of our lives. Of late, I have been very fortunate to find new elements of Catholicism that resonate in my heart. Pope Francis is a gift to the Catholic Church and to the world. He is building many bridges that are allowing all human beings to be true to who they are.

There is a general belief that everyone within a religion or organization thinks and believes in the same dogma. Furthermore, it often is assumed that a group of people who belong to the same institution hold identical beliefs, and blindly make the same judgments that condone or condemn others' actions or situations. Fortunately, some people exist in our world who defy any such classification. These persons, who cannot be grouped under a general belief or category, are the outliers. The man, whom I am about to speak of, is known throughout our world for his teachings and the connections that he has created worldwide. His name is Father Thomas Keating.

As a world-renowned author, a monk, and a priest, he is a blessing to our world. In the fall of 2015, I had the privilege and honor to meet Thomas Keating and was able to speak with him, one on one. Though we spent only a little more than an hour together, that meeting has left indelible impressions on me.

One of the first things that I said to him was, "My brother and his partner just got married." I guess I was trying to gauge who he was through his reaction and/or response. Do you know what he said? *"That is wonderful, Cyrina!"* There was zero judgment. I was shocked because I was not expecting him to be so accepting and loving. Taken aback, I said to him, "You are a Catholic priest, right? That is not what the church taught us in Catholic school." He smiled, and with sincerity, simply said, *"Cyrina, it is all about love."*

His words, so simple yet so profound, made my heart open up to him. I felt happy and thankful to hear a Catholic priest say those words. At the end of our visit, I asked him if he would be open to me taking a picture of us together. He said sure and asked, *"Will this be a selfie?"* Such a hip, 92 years young priest!

This time with Thomas Keating made me feel so grateful because it has opened my eyes in many ways. I saw some situations and conditions in our world in a new light for the first time in my life. I have known that there are people who are limiting and stick to such beliefs for reasons unknown to me. However, I now know that other people have chosen to expand their minds and hearts to become more accepting and loving. The truth is we do not know the ins and outs of another's life. If we try to come from a place of love, not judgment, we can build more bridges and connections with others. We must learn to listen with open minds to understand others' perspectives, for that is the only way to open so many closed judgmental doors. I encourage people to adopt mindsets and actions that embrace expansion, not constriction.

I am very thankful to have Tim as my brother-in-law; excited and happy that Justin has found a wonderful partner. My brothers are twins. I used to tease them by saying that they would be ideal for a science project since one is straight and the other is gay. There is the question out there: *Is being gay a choice or part of someone's physiology?* In my mind, this illustrates that it is in our physiology. I hope there will be a day in the near future that people will allow themselves to be true to who they are. We all have a similar, although different, biology, and we, as a society, need to grow and expand with acceptance for our differences. The Bullard family definitely walks on nontraditional paths.

Returning to turning 40 years young, my birthday celebration made for a great night. My friend, Kerri, had made a beautiful tri-level German Chocolate cake...my favorite! The night was filled with lots of laughter, joy, big hugs, and love. Many of my friends had made a huge effort to celebrate with me, and we all had a good time together. It was more beautiful because we were with each other and on the same frequency of happiness. Being very thankful, I truly wanted to live.

With this birthday, I became much more in tune with the meaning of the "gift of life," and how many of us take this gift for granted! Life definitely can get crazy and challenging at times. Life may start to feel like we are on a roller coaster ride with its unexpected dips and turns. Having experienced these highs and lows of life, I have discovered some tools that we can use to keep ourselves grounded. One tool is contemplative prayer, based on teachings brought to us by Father Thomas Keating; these have elevated the honor I felt to have met him.

I started daily contemplative prayer in January of 2016. I call my practice RPM, an acronym for Rest, Pee, and Meditate. It is the first thing I do in the morning, and feel it has brought more calmness, centeredness, and connectedness into my life! I encourage others to practice contemplative prayer, meditation or mindfulness to help to bring more calmness.

The science behind these practices is expanding. These practices can help to restore our connections in life, whether it is the feeling of being connected with our Self, our surroundings, or our higher power. Many scientifically proven benefits are linked to meditation. With the multiple types of meditations available, you are likely to come across a type that will resonate with you. Some of the findings and benefits of meditation include extended longevity, as well as the management and prevention of anxiety. Meditation creates a state of reducing reactiveness. It also increases your clarity of thinking, improves focus, increases the grey matter in the brain, and improves the immune system. These are just a few of the benefits that you can have with meditation!

During Pharmacy School, I never learned anything about the science behind meditation or all the potential benefits that can be generated from its practice. We need to accept the fact that challenges will always come our way. However, we can equip ourselves with effective tools for our toolbox, implementing their use for meeting life's challenges more successfully than we have done in the past. Specifically, I feel that we need to teach our youth how to practice meditation. It can help them to deal better with daily living and how this can allow them to maintain calmness when dealing with challenges that, unfortunately, are inevitable. The Dalai Lama says "*If every 8-year-old in the world is taught meditation, we will eliminate violence from the world within one generation.*"

It is interesting how fast life can progress. My 40th birthday had been a celebration of my upcoming journey, traveling into my 5th decade! The majority of the time, I am thankful for the circumstances that have occurred in my life. Through these experiences, I have learned to be more present in my life by living in the moment. I do feel that allowing myself to celebrate my daily journey brings more happiness, meaning, and gratitude into my life. This is something that we can all do if we want our lives to be more meaningful and happy.

Takeaway Lessons from this Chapter:

* Life is a gift; allow gratitude and celebration!

* Family and friends are blessings, who can help you along your journey.

* With any organization, there are outliers who do not align with everything the organization believes. Try not to take just the blanket beliefs, which can be overgeneralized, or you can miss the impactful nuances that are present.

* Meditation can have a very positive impact on our lives. Practicing it is well worth the investment of time.

* "It is all about love."

* The most conscious connection created in this chapter of my life was reconnecting with my friends. On my 40th birthday being able to celebrate my life and my friendships was a huge gift!

* What connections were created for you in Chapter 9?

Chapter 10

Tree of Life

It was time for a visit from Scott. Who is Scott, you may ask? He had been a very significant man in my life. In fact, he is the first man I ever fell in love with, which magnifies his significance! It had been quite some time since I had seen him. And now, he was coming to visit me! I was really nervous about seeing him, but at the same time, extremely excited. Despite all the conflicting feelings, I wanted to see this man, whom I called the first love of my life!

How Scott came to have such an important place in my life is a very interesting story. He and I met in 2004 in the city of Chicago. As you can see, it has been many, many years since we had first met. When I first got to know him, never could I have predicted that he would play such a significant role in my life. We have always had a long-distance relationship, not optimal, but worth the challenge, at least in my mind. Probably you would think that the physical distance would have gotten in the way and restricted how we both felt about each other. From my point of view, I can say that the distance did not define my feelings for him. I felt very connected to him and had also been very stimulated by him in multiple ways!

Scott is a very intelligent and funny guy who can be goofy sometimes. In addition, Scott is well-endowed in many ways, and I found him extremely attractive. When he visited me this time, I had not seen him in a few years, although he was still as handsome as ever. He arrived at my home with a huge bag filled with very thoughtful and silly gifts. Each one of those small presents brought lots of laughter and smiles.

He was the ex-boyfriend my family had not allowed to visit me when I was in the hospital. This was because they were unsure of the kind of emotional impact his presence would have on me. Once I was able to make my own decisions, I accepted his offer to visit. Often, I wonder about the role of people in one's life when they are placed on our path. There are times when I look at the individuals who are a part of my life, and the thought pops in my head, "Why are they in my life?"

While Scott has brought a lot of positive things to my world, he has also brought a lot of heartache and pain! During his visit, we had spent time with friends of mine and time alone. He had gotten along well with my friends, and our time together had been filled with laughter.

During this time, I had been going through some extreme shifts concerning the functioning of my body, brain, mind, and heart. I was feeling very vulnerable and self-conscious. Now I was the owner of a tracheotomy scar and two very long thin scars on my back. I was afraid he would no longer be attracted to me.

One night, our kissing gave me very positive feelings, indicating that we were not going to stay on first base. Feeling very nervous, I decided to take off my shirt and show him the scars on my back before we got too carried away.

I wanted to gauge his reaction. I said, "If these scars turn you off, I do not want to be intimate because they are not going to leave my body." Hugging me, and kissing my neck, he told me that the scars did not bother him. These words and his loving response, both verbal and physical, made me feel confident to move forward. Game on! I was proud of the fact that I had allowed myself to be vulnerable, despite all my fears.

Eventually, we moved to a home run! This was such a relief to move forward and to realize I could still have an orgasm! With Vitamin O still available to me, I was beyond ecstatic! Not only did I have sex with a hot guy, but I'd had an orgasm. Yahoo! With a spinal cord injury, you never know what parts of your body it will impact. Often, I have felt that this time with Scott had been a significant part of my life. This time was a vital juncture for me. I had been gifted with a very beneficial contribution, and this had developed into a meaningful visit. At least for me, it had been significant and special.

Too soon, it was time for Scott to head back to Ohio. I will never forget that day; October 25, was very significant for him, as it was the yearly observance of his mother's death. Personally, I know these are always grievous days, as March 28th is the anniversary of my father's death. This day is invariably painful for me. Fortunately, my father is always in my heart, especially on that day.

Scott and I had driven together to the airport. My friend Julie was flying into Denver on that day as well. Scott and I hugged and kissed good-bye. Yes, I was on cloud nine; the visit had turned out so well. In fact, it had been much better than I had expected!

It was unfortunate that Scott and Julie were not able to meet at the airport. Jules and I have been friends forever since the eighth grade. We grew up in a small city, Deland, Florida, which is the skydiving capital of the world, our claim to fame!

It is interesting how two people can have such different paths and still feel completely connected to each other. My friend Julie Anderson grew up to become a supermodel, and I had become a pharmacist. She had just moved back to the States from Paris a few weeks before she came to visit. I felt so thankful that she came to Colorado to see me. Julie has three children, and I adore all of them! Although we led very different lives, we still have remained connected throughout our lives. I was so excited and grateful to have had this chance to hang out with Jules. It was a good feeling to be with a friend who has been walking on my path with me for many years.

When Julie was here, we had taken an adventure day to enjoy The Republic of Boulder. I lived in this beautiful city from 1995 till 1999, about three and a half years. Since I have been a resident, I can say that, although beautiful, it's a little extreme! Here's a joke that I like to share: *when I relocated to Colorado this time, I moved to Denver because Boulder is too extreme. They have extreme athletes, extreme pot smokers, and extreme crystal worshipers!* With that said, it is an amazingly beautiful, eclectic, alternative city to visit. Julie and I had a lovely day, filled with fun and adventures in Boulder.

One night, we met my friend Jen, who was the co-owner of my home. It was so nice to be with two good friends, one who had known me for 27 years, and the other for 14 years. The three of us had a lot of laughs together and had a delightful bonding night. Of course, the hot topic of conversation had been Scott's visit and what I thought about the possibility of an "us!" I was trying to be present in the moment with my friends, although I felt a bit distracted. The distraction came from my being slightly consumed with the subsequent feelings of Scott's recent visit. I was optimistic about a potential future with Scott.

As a female, it is always a challenge not to allow one's self to be overly hopeful in the building of a future together with someone. We like to paint a beautiful picture, even when we do not have all the necessary colors. Scott and I had dated on three different occasions since we had met. During all of the time we spent together, I could not help but feel that Scott was married to his job. It wasn't that he didn't give me any attention; it just was that I could see that his work always came first. Scott knew what I wanted in my life because I had never made it a secret. During his recent visit, I had assumed he had been present with me because he wanted the same things that I did. I thought that he had seen the same potential future with me that I had seen with him. No one ever knows how a relationship will develop or where the journey will take you. I must continue to welcome unanticipated options from various possibilities and not close myself off.

My visit with Jules had come to an end, and I was sad to see her go. Now I was going to be on my own. While I did have my housemate, Melissa, we did not see each other all of the time. Hence, I was going to make the most of these new circumstances. Ready to spread my wings, I was going to spend time alone. I intended to allow myself to have the strength and determination to own my independence.

Fortunately, I had tremendous insurance through my employment because the bills from this one accident had accumulated to about one million dollars! Health care is imperative; and, I recognize that if I did not have good medical insurance, my life would be very different today. Relatively young individuals who do not have a family, usually do not think about Long Term Disability Insurance. Thank God, I chose a plan that had LTD benefits!

This insurance was one of the best investments I have ever made. Its importance is second only to the lifesaving flip flops! The healing process after the surgery took a long time. Thankfully, I was being paid as I journeyed through these transitions of healing physically, mentally, and emotionally. I was on a mission to regain my independence. Financially, I knew I was going to be fine; I would not have to request monetary assistance or compensation. However, I did have to ask for many other favors, such as rides to the grocery store and other activities, as well as help lifting heavy things. I needed to have people spend time with me, but never their money. Thankfully, I had that one covered!

Before my accident, I was a salaried pharmacist, whose pay was based on 22 hours of work a week. Those 22 hours were usually 26 to 28 in actuality. I'm sure you know how salaried positions operate; the employee always works more hours, never less. At least in the healthcare world, this is the standard.

I was making enough money to pay my bills and save a little; I wasn't making a ton, although doing well. During the fall before my accident, I had decided to increase my work schedule to 36 hours a week, because I had wanted to adopt a child. I love children, and always thought I would be married and have children! My path in life, however, had not followed my assumption. The new plan was to save for a year; then I would make the leap and adopt a child. Unfortunately, my accident had thrown a wrench into that plan. And now, my path was looking very different from the one I had imagined.

When I used my disability insurance benefits, my monthly payments were based on 36 working hours a week, not 22. I could only say to myself, "What a Godsend!" I was truly fortunate to be making the increased amount because it allowed me to take baby steps returning to work. Slow and steady was how I planned to return to my regular work week, as suggested by Craig Hospital. With the LTD insurance, I was able to implement the plan recommended to me without being financially penalized.

So, with the worry about finances on the back burner, I could celebrate the many ordinary, everyday things I could do on my own after my accident. Others might find them to be small things, but for me, they were huge victories! Slowly and surely, I was gaining my independence back. The first time I drove a car by myself was a huge undertaking!

Craig Hospital has a fantastic program to help their patients to resume driving. This was another major part of my independence. Colleen had been fantastic; she helped me hone my skills to prepare me for the practical part of my driving test at the DMV.

Many times, while I was driving with her, I thought of her as my friend, not my instructor. My neurologist had encouraged my family and me to go to an empty parking lot to practice there. Finally, the day came when I was to go to the DMV to take the written and driving tests. Michael, a former boyfriend, and my *"Knight in Shining Hummer®,"* drove me to the DMV for my testing.

Michael had gained this unique title many years prior, and it relates to the story of how we met. Coming back from a day of skiing, when I was driving eastbound on I-70, I hit black ice. My car spun out of control on this major highway and I ended up on the median. This was an extremely scary experience that had my heart pumping like crazy, while desperately trying to calm down. Thankfully, I had not hurt anyone or myself, a miracle in and of itself on such a busy highway.

At the same time, Michael had been driving westbound in a bright yellow Hummer®. He was so generous to stop and help me. He had been able to pull my car out of the sunken median with the strength of his Hummer®. Needless to say, I was very thankful for his help! He asked for my phone number, saying that he wanted to make sure I got home safely, or so I thought. Keep in mind, I was not a fashion plate that day, as I was in my bulky ski clothes and my hair looked a mess. More importantly, I am sure I was as white as a ghost when he first saw me. Surprisingly, shortly after being helped by the Knight in the Shining Hummer®, he and I started to date.

As life is a continual roller coaster, our relationship did not last. Michael is a wonderful friend to me now. There had been a period of time when we did not talk because of the negative feelings that had developed between us after our breakup. Thankfully, he is now very present in my life, although our relationship is strictly platonic. Today, he is a loyal and faithful Christian, and his growth has been tremendous over the years. After we had broken up, he gave me this poem. I was taken aback by this gesture since he wrote this poem when he was dating someone else. Timing is very interesting! Here are his beautiful words:

Pulse of the World

There was magic the day you were born

A friend to all new and worn

A blessing to the world for all to see

Truth and compassion and consistency

One fateful day, when your end was near

I happened upon you, your eyes like a deer

In the ditch you were sitting, sweat in your palm

I was there in a flash, to bring you calm

I am honored to know you, one of a kind

Making life fun, you're quite the find

A special person, you have become

Giving life a buzz, like a bottle of rum

No stranger exists, in the world, you live

Every person you meet, a handshake you give

Your smile and your laugh, infectious they are

In every corner of the world, it is never too far.

I thank the stars, for becoming your friend

Your knowledge and wisdom, they never end

You are the model of loyalty, truth to the core

Making people feel like royalty, without ever a chore

The world has energy, and I know it is you

Never alone and never blue

From north to south and east to west

You are a friend that I would call the best

Happy Birthday ~ September 12, 2006

Michael

So thankful to have received such a thoughtful and meaningful poem. It is fascinating how we first met, the many things that we have been through together, and how years later, he continues to be an important, positive person in my life. Relationships, they say, can be for a season, a reason or a lifetime. I am certain my Knight in Shining Hummer®, and I will be friends for a lifetime.

When I went to the DMV, it was December of 2010, and I was nervous. I so wanted to be able to drive again...to gain that part of my independence back. I had gotten a 100% on the written test and done well on the practical. In the end, I passed! This was my first written and graded test since I had been diagnosed with a traumatic brain injury. The fact that I got 100% was huge! Yes, I realize it is not rocket science, although it was significant for me. This accomplishment granted me another leap towards my independence. I had become so motivated to do more!

Regaining my ability to drive opened up many doors that had closed after my accident. I could finally be more in control of my schedule, instead of depending on other people or the Regional Transportation District (RTD) schedule. Driving is another activity that I believe many of us take for granted; we expect to be able to drive wherever and whenever we want. For me, being able to drive opened the door to returning to work. I started to talk with Tiffany at Craig Hospital about creating a plan for my reintegration into the workforce.

The process has been another very significant milestone in my recovery! I had accomplished tons of rehabilitation goals as well as having worked as an intern at the Craig Hospital Pharmacy. Now I felt confident that I would not only excel at my career, but I would make a positive impact on my patients and the community.

Baby steps were the basis of the plan that Tiffany and I created together. The store where I worked had a fantastic team; the supervisors were very supportive. Their help allowed me to achieve a slow transition and integration back into my career. My employer and I worked with Craig Hospital to make my experience as successful as possible. People often dive into returning to work too quickly; in fact, they rush. Unfortunately, this often ends up moving them backward rather than forward. I have been so grateful that I allowed Craig Hospital and Tiffany to guide me in this process. Going back to work would be a slow and steady process. Purposefully not rushing it; I wanted to be successful!

We began to plan the first steps for returning to work with only two four-hour shifts per week. It surprised me that I felt so exhausted after only a four-hour shift of work. Prior to the accident, I worked 12 to 14 consecutive hours without feeling exhausted. This made me feel grateful that I had not taken too much on too soon. Thank goodness I had the guidance available at the right time!

In general, I have been a very driven person. This accident made me put on the brakes. After my bike accident, fatigue has been prevalent in my world. During the recovery process after my accident, I definitely took advantage of an overdose of this medicine called sleep. This is a very common symptom for a TBI patient. A pharmacist must be extremely focused, present, and aware. Sleep is so important for all of us, it gives time for our bodies to recover from the stress placed on our bodies during the day. For all of us, it is one of the best medicines in the world!

Thankfully, my supervisors were keenly helpful. They scheduled me with another pharmacist for many of my shifts to make sure I was supported and to make the transition as smooth as possible. I realized that it was going to be a slow and steady process. I was thankful that I was beginning to catch potential drug interactions and errors and making a positive impact on the patients, their lives, and their healthcare.

My confidence was coming back. I was going to be okay and going to be able to make a positive impact on my patients' lives and in my community. So thankful to be moving in the right direction. I had really missed my patients while I was gone. Many times, I joked with the moms and dads at the pharmacy, saying, "I remember when you were pregnant and when your child was born, now, your child is going into the fourth grade. The children are getting older, although we are not, right?" I felt beyond thankful for the patient relationships I had built.

Children are a true indicator of how fast time goes. I have found it really satisfying to have built these relationships with my patients and to have known their whole family. A few of my patients shared that their children felt special when I remembered their names. Since I do not have children of my own, I hope that I am making a positive impact on the future by helping these children feel happy about their interactions with adults.

I love the relationships that I built with most of the patients at the pharmacy. A few of them knew what had occurred. Others said to me things like: *I missed you. Where did you go? Did you have a baby?* This made for an interesting transition back to work. Since I was very cautious about what and with whom I shared my story, only a few close and trusted patients knew what had happened.

Most individuals do not want to hear that their pharmacist, who is now back at work dispensing their medication, had a TBI. This has been a delicate road for me to maneuver. Slowly I increased my hours to 22 hours a week, salaried. This, as I shared before, is really around 26 hours of actual working time. Eventually getting back into my groove at work, I was gaining more independence. And, reconnecting with my patients and colleagues gave me a sense of confidence.

Eventually, I was back to work with full force; however, still only working 22 hours because of the fatigue. At times, I would have to take leave of absence and use my LTD again. Standing for 10-13 hours a day, with only a 10 to 20-minute break, can cause really grim effects on the back. The rods and screws in my back exacerbated this.

At times, I was also dealing with sleep issues. It is never an option to be a pharmacist and not get enough sleep, especially with a history of a traumatic brain injury. In this career, I am expected to be focused and knowledgeable; because people's lives are in my hands.

To feel better, I had to take a few leaves of absence from work. Again, feeling so blessed to have the LTD. Never had I thought I would have to deal with such prolonged challenges in my life. Now I am moving through it and learning every step of the way. Many unpredictable things have happened on my journey. I think this fact reinforces the need to be in the moment, to be present, and to enjoy life because no one ever knows what tomorrow holds.

I had worked at the same pharmacy since June of 2004. That pharmacy is located in a small town with lovely people. I truly connected with many of the patients, and that allowed me to call them my friends. It is like a small-town community pharmacy.

My baby steps back to work started on January 25th, 2011. I had transitioned back to my 22-hour a week shift by the end of May 2011, which was the time of the first anniversary of the bicycle accident. At times, when I think of this process, it seems surreal, going through so many huge changes in such a short period of time. Most of all, reminding myself, life has no guarantees, and to make sure I enjoy the daily ride!

Takeaway Lessons from this Chapter:

※ First loves have a special place in our hearts.

※ Baby steps are important; so is celebrating the small victories along the way.

※ Supportive friends from the eighth grade, always have a place in your heart.

※ The "Knight in Shining Hummer®" who was so helpful will always be on the friend list.

※ Passing the DMV test can be a huge victory.

※ LTD is a worthwhile investment, as you never know the course of your life's journey.

※ The connections you make at work can be meaningful and inspiring.

※ The most conscious connection created in this chapter of my life was reconnecting with my first love. My time with Scott was exciting and allowed many wonderful feelings to resurface in my life.

※ What connections were created for you in Chapter 10?

Chapter 11

Important Men

Another major celebration in my life was close on the horizon: the first anniversary of my accident. This was major because it marked another extremely significant occurrence in my life. The previous year had been overflowing with my attempts to embrace my losses, to overcome the seemingly endless hurdles, and to regain my independence. Slowly, I had been settling back into my personal life while striving to become re-acclimated to my professional life.

Additionally, it was Memorial Day weekend, and I was going to run the Bolder Boulder, an annual tradition with my friends, Debbie and Larry, and their daughters, Molly and Amy. Finally, and probably the biggest cause for celebration was that I could have a glass of wine! It had been a little over one year since I had even had a drop of alcohol. Now it was time for me to celebrate with libations.

The planning for this anniversary celebration started a month before the festivities. At this time, I was still dating Scott. We were having a great time together. During this period of time, we met in Colorado, Ohio his home state, and we had also met in Santa Fe for a fun getaway. Being together again meant a lot to me. I was feeling very excited about our relationship and our future!

The relationship with Scott, my first love, was progressing and we were reconnecting. This time around, I had accepted in my heart that we were going to get married and have children. Scott knew that this was the intention of the path that I held in my heart. A month before the party, I called Scott with the specific intent of having a heart to heart talk. This was not going to be easy because it never is. Knowing that I was going to feel nervous, I was cognizant of how much I needed answers to some very important questions. Along with my joyful expectations, I had all these nagging doubts. The question that needed to be answered was, *"Where do you think we are going in our relationship?"*

Scott and I had been involved on and off for about eight years. For this reason, I felt there should not be any indecision. Convinced I knew his convictions because those answers were already in my head. Also, my ovaries were screaming: "IT IS TIME!"

When I finally mustered up the courage to have this conversation with Scott, he first explained that he cared deeply about me and loved me. Then he added that at this point in his life, he neither wanted to get married nor to have children.

Shocked to hear his words, this certainly was not what I had expected. I thought to myself, why did this man who claimed he loved me not let me know how he felt before getting back into a relationship with me? Why in the world had he come back into my life knowing what I wanted? Why did he want to f**k with my head? Hey dude, I have already had a traumatic brain injury! I was crushed...and pissed!

Obviously, I did not invite him to my one-year anniversary party. Making this decision to let go was very hard, yet I could not ignore what his clear answers had indicated. I must let him go. It did not help that I felt like an idiot, somewhat delusional, and deceived. Furthermore, I knew it was going to take considerable work and time to heal.

The one-year anniversary party day finally arrived! This celebration had been arranged around so many events. I began the day by running the Bolder Boulder, a fun annual event, and a group tradition for some friends and me. This year held much more significance for me, due to my life-threatening accident just one year before. I was excited that I was even able to run!

Established in 1979, the Bolder Boulder is a huge annual race, marked by contagiously positive energy from over 50,000 participants and tons of spectators. Being present at this event allowed me to experience all the positive energy associated with the Bolder Boulder.

This time my goal was to be able to run the entire race without stopping. This was a huge endeavor since I had had spine surgery less than one year before the race. I was able to complete a 10 K (6.2 miles) run without stopping. I was beyond psyched that I had been successful in my mission! I certainly had not finished fast; even so, this was a huge victory for me! Once again, I realized my ability to accomplish what I set out to do. Now clear that when I focus my mind, my heart, and my soul on a mission, it can come to fruition. After the race, I went home to start preparing for the festivities.

My brother, Jason, who was living in Boulder at the time, brought one of his friends and came to help me get ready for the festivities. I had invited so many people over to celebrate and have a drink with me! The invitation list also included all of my doctors, therapists, and some of the staff from Craig Hospital. My spine surgeon and physical therapist both came, as well as many friends; I felt so supported and loved that day. My heart was full!

My sister had sent a nice bottle of red wine, *"The Prisoner."* I felt this was an appropriate selection for the year that I had just lived through because I felt like a prisoner at times. But now, it was time, and I was ready to spread my wings and be free. This was going to be my first taste of alcohol in over a year. I gathered seven of my best girlfriends together to open the bottle. We celebrated the day, as well as our friendship.

Within our friendships, each of us had experienced challenges in life. Yet, we had helped one another move through the tough times, helping each other to be able to overcome our obstacles. Up until this point, I had generally taken on the role of a giver, but something had shifted. Due to the events that had unfolded that year, I had been forced by circumstances to become more of a taker. Life is a balance, and it became crucial for me to be a receiver to move through this part of my life successfully.

I was honored that Dr. Henderhiser, my spine surgeon, had come to the celebration. I was able to introduce him to Stefan, my friend and physical therapist (PT), who specializes in the spine. Now they refer patients to each other and have developed a professional relationship. A few other people came from Craig Hospital, as well. I felt very connected to all of my guests. Surrounded by all these loving people, who sent only positive vibes my way, I can say that this was one of the most wonderful days of my life.

It did not take long to feel the effects of the alcohol. After only two glasses, I began to feel very relaxed. In fact, you could say that my liquid confidence was flowing. The party was a considerable success for everyone who attended! There was a lot of laughter, great company, and fantastic food.

I was so honored by the turnout. I have many wonderful memories to keep from that day. This had been a year filled with challenges, humility, hard work, emotional pain, physical pain, fear, tears, disappointment, intermixed with celebrations, spiritual awakenings, and love. I can say that at this time in my life, I have learned lessons that will last me forever.

During this year, two very important men had been brought into my world. Mark, who lives in Vail, was my first responder. I am forever grateful to him. It had been a year and a half after my accident before I was finally able to connect with him. I wanted to take him to dinner to

THANK him for saving my life! When he took me up on my offer, I asked him to choose any restaurant in Vail. He chose a place that was offering a deal: buy one meal, get the second for 50% off. Laughing, I said to him, "you did not have to pick a place with a good deal". Mark smiled and said, *"I chose it because I like this restaurant."* When we sat at our table, he remarked, *"You look very different from the last time I saw you."* Of course, I had to make a joke by answering, "Oh, I forgot to bring the blood and dirt!" Together, we had a good laugh.

Mark was able to shed light on what had occurred that day and to help me make sense of it all. He shared with me that, while I was riding on the path, the front tire of my bike went off the path onto the soft sand. My feet were clipped into the pedals and I started to do extreme gymnastics or complicated somersaults, while my bike was still attached to me. Thankfully, Mark stopped to help me. Immediately, he recognized that I was not responsive, and he began CPR. Fortunately, Mark had been trained in CPR as part of a first responder's course in the wilderness. I was the first person whom he had ever used his skills on.

His training had been expensive, although his father told him, *"That's the best $5,000 I have ever spent!"* I was very touched by that statement. Mark's father, whom I had never met, had such an appreciation for his son saving my life, while I felt such deep gratitude for Mark. After dinner, we went for a coffee to continue our heartfelt conversation. By the end of the evening, I felt very connected, enlightened, and even more grateful. I finally had the opportunity to put a face to the name of the man who had saved my life!

I drove Mark back to his car, and we said goodnight. Mark gently held my hand and kissed it before he said, *"I love you."* Somewhat taken aback, I said, "I love you, too, and I am so grateful to you for my life." This love was obviously not romantic or lustful love; it was the love of one human being for another. Without Mark, I would not be alive today. His compassionate act made me wonder, *how will I stand up if life places such an intense situation on my path*?

Trevor Hart is the other very impactful and important man who had been introduced into my world that year, for a reason! My time with him has been an enlightening and eye-opening gift. I mentioned him earlier, as he has been my intuitive healer, and I was his first traumatic brain injury client. He now is an intuitive healer for famous people; I have joked with him and said, "Trevor, please do not forget the little people."

After being discharged from Craig Hospital, I continued to work with Trevor. At first, Trevor was able to do sessions with me via phone.

Later, when I had recovered enough to be able to drive, I had the privilege of meeting him in person. His office was in Louisville, Colorado, where I would have 90-minute intuitive healing sessions. The time that he spent working with me has continued to be of benefit and has been healing. After Trevor moved out of state, I stopped having sessions with him. I no longer work with him except for extreme situations. When a close relative of mine was battling Non-Hodgkin's Lymphoma, I hired him to work remotely with her. Thankfully, she has been in remission since 2014. Trevor and his wife, Sharon, are working together to bring wonderful things to our world. Their website is: lightbodyengineering.com

Western medicine needs to become open to treating patients with more than just standardized procedures and medications. Thank God, we have access to more expansive beliefs and alternative practices today! There are so many other therapies that can be introduced to the medical world, which complement the traditional modes of therapy. I am living proof that different healing modalities are very beneficial! Fortunately, many hospitals are now adopting massage therapy, acupuncture, music therapy, and art therapy, to name a few.

Escape Fire: The Fight to Rescue American Healthcare is a film by Susan Froemke and Matthew Heineman. An extremely alarming documentary, it illustrates many of the challenges faced by the healthcare system in America. The documentary is somber and somewhat scary, but at the same time extremely enlightening. For anyone who takes the time to watch this movie, I think it will be shocking and eye-opening. I do realize that money is important; however, choosing money over health isn't wise. Money should not be the primary deciding factor when it comes to improving the quality and standards of healthcare.

Personally, I hope that the healthcare system in America evolves and embraces different healing modalities. I would love to see our world of health norms transform to become one that starts with preventative measures at a very young age. This is the mindset that must be adopted, instead of having to put on multiple Band-Aids® later in life. I would love it if we could introduce practices of meditation and more exercise; teach children how to garden, cook and eat healthily; and practice yoga. This could also include teaching how we can deal with emotions using HeartMath® tools and introduce different systems and effective techniques for the use of Conversational Intelligence® to help create communication that builds trust.

Furthermore, many books could be added to mandatory reading lists for high school students, specifically, books by Judith Glaser, Brené

Brown, and Mel Robbins. These three authors have much to offer, as their books give the reader the necessary tools for developing better coping and communication skills.

Judith Glaser's, *Conversational Intelligence: How Great Leaders Build Trust and Get Extraordinary Results* is a book with major insight into and tools to elevate the effectiveness of our conversations. She shared with her readers different ways to effectively use Conversational Intelligence® to facilitate good communication to optimize outcomes.

Brené Brown's *Rising Strong* is a compelling book that can help us be brave and rise when we are knocked down by our struggles. Dr. Brown is a professor at The University of Houston, as well as the author of several insightful books. Investing time to read her books, I feel, will help facilitate authenticity in our world.

Another very insightful book I want to include is *The 5 Second Rule: Transform your Life, Work, and Confidence with Everyday Courage* by Mel Robbins, a lawyer and now a talk show host. Being a pharmacist, I find it fascinating that Robbins's anxiety had been treated with medication for twenty years. Now, by using her 5-second rule tool, she has been able to discontinue the medication and effectively deal with her anxiety. Her book has helped many people! Thankfully, because of the impact of her book, people have decided not to commit suicide. They have chosen to move forward and have a positive impact on our world!

I thank each of these authors for the amazing gifts that they have shared with our world. With that said, none of these books are to take the place of healthcare. When an individual has a hard time (physically, mentally, spiritually, and psychologically), professional counseling, medical care, or both, is necessary. Still, the ideas and techniques in these phenomenal books, when incorporated into a person's life, offers helpful tools to develop coping and communication skills. Adding these to our toolbox can give us a myriad of tools to deal more effectively and successfully with life and the obstacles that can be thrown on our paths.

Takeaway Lessons from this Chapter:

❉ There is light after dark, challenging times.

❉ Support and love can help you to spread your wings and soar high.

❋ Select the right tools; they are the ones that help you elevate and to move you forward on your life journey.

❋ Permit yourself to move through these challenges to allow for growth and evolution in your life.

❋ Do not ignore or suppress pain. Embrace and release it and move through its challenge.

❋ Establishing if you are on the same page in a relationship may save you precious time, as well as pain.

❋ The most conscious connection created in this chapter of my life was to meet Mark. This meeting with the man who saved my life shed light on my accident and how wonderful people can be!

❋ What connections were created for you in Chapter 11?

Chapter 12

Serendipity

The challenges I have faced in this year of my life have been enlightening. They have allowed me to become more present, reflective, and spiritual. Some days we are just rushing from one thing to the next. This is unfortunate because we do not grant ourselves a pause to take inventory of the beauty, possibilities, and gifts placed on our path. At times, events occur in our lives that force us to put on the brakes and take a look at the situation at hand. It is then that we may become more grateful. When we allow ourselves to be open and let serendipity shine, new elements can enter into our worlds. Where do we start?

Being female brings a level of self-consciousness into my life; unfortunately, I am very much acquainted with this feeling. Today, on my back, I wear two long thin scars that have introduced a new element of insecurity into my world! They should be my badge of honor, my warrior wounds, and a victory stamp. However, insecurities still creep in about my scars. Larry, a.k.a. Dr. Barfield, is one of my Bolder Boulder buddies. I have been friends with him and his family since 1996. Dr. Barfield, a dermatologist, happens to be a very generous person. His assistant performed free laser therapy on my back scars. Otherwise, this procedure would have been cost-prohibitive and not justifiable for me. Although the laser did not remove the scars, it did make them fainter and less noticeable. I was so blessed to have such a thoughtful friend in my life.

The second person on this serendipitous gift chain was Stefan, who became my physical therapist after my release from care at Craig Hospital. Stefan and I have been friends since 1998. When I was in his office, I said, "We have been friends for 12 years, and now my spine has decided I should become your patient. Wow!" I had first met Stefan through a mutual friend who lived in Florida. When I met him, he was on the path to becoming a monk. Later, Stefan had a shift in his plans; he had gone on a retreat and met Theresa. That was when his "monkhood" went out the window, and he chose "husbandhood" instead. Theresa and Stefan have been married for years and have two wonderful children.

One Sunday, months after my accident, Stefan decided to introduce me to the church where he and his wife are members. I went and discovered a service like no other I had attended in the past! By the end of the service, I was bawling my eyes out. This church and its message resonated so deeply with me and my heart, I was instantly confident this was where I was supposed to be. Also, I have taken several classes there and have participated in some workshops. The church has hosted amazing speakers, including Dr. Eben Alexander, Dr. Deepak Chopra, Dr. Wayne Dyer, Anita Moorjani, and Dr. Christiane Northrup that I have seen speak. My world was opening, and I have been on a spiritual journey ever since!

I have called myself a recovering Catholic, so I find it funny that Stefan, who was going to be a monk in the Catholic Church, introduced me to the *Mile Hi, Science of the Mind Church*. I love Mile Hi, as their messages make me want to be a better person. They do not teach about guilt, those ingrained feelings from my childhood. My experiences on my journey at this church have really allowed me to feel more connected and to grow in the spiritual realm.

Stefan was also the one who introduced me to Father Thomas Keating, the Catholic monk and priest. Father Thomas is the gentleman who said, *"Cyrina, it is all about love."* The more I think about this statement and relate it to the basics in life, the more I understand it to be the truth. As a result, I am trying to surround myself with love, positive people, and experiences, while saying goodbye to the energy vampires. There is a fantastic documentary about the life of Thomas Keating called *The Rising Tide of Silence*. Unfortunately, Father Thomas passed away on October 25, 2018. I was so grateful to have had the opportunity to have met him. He blessed the world with his presence and teachings that he shared. He was friends with the Dalai Lama and other spiritual leaders from all around the world; one could say that he was very well-connected! He studied the mystics and helped reintroduce contemplative prayer to the world. I am so thankful to have taken a few courses in Denver about contemplative prayer. This form of prayer is a meditation that allows dedicated time to connect with God. For those who have other beliefs, in my mind, this is time to connect with the divine, Buddha, the Universe (whatever word you would like to use, for the higher power) as well as connecting with yourself. The time for contemplative prayer is when you can be present, centered, and calm: "just be."

Earlier I shared information about meditation, although I feel it is crucial for me to impress the incredible impact it can have once again. Even though I am a recovering Catholic, I have been practicing contemplative prayer every morning for a little more than four years. Still learning how to be present and trying not to let my mind travel all around the place, some days are more successful than others. This practice has helped to keep me grounded. Being silent is not my strong suit, although I embrace it; I am learning to stop exercising my mouth. I feel that this is an expansive part of my journey.

Through science, we now know that meditation has a positive impact on our physiology, our lives, as well as our brains. It allows us to be more present and in the moment. It can help our ability to focus and have a positive effect on our immune system. Meditation can improve our emotional well-being by decreasing depression and anxiety while allowing more happiness in our world. It can benefit the brain by increasing grey matter. Moreover, another widely acclaimed aspect of this practice is that there are no side effects associated with meditation, at least to my knowledge. Being in the moment has been a huge lesson for me. I found that being present is something that can help to facilitate my happiness instead of worrying about the future or regretting the past. With that said, I encourage everyone to take baby steps and find what provides the best benefits.

My heart had become heavy at work because I was dispensing anti-anxiety medication to teenagers, knowing life was not going to get easier. Being medicated at a young age for anxiety, what did this mean for the future of these young people? I was introduced to HeartMath® through research and talking to friends. HeartMath has over 25 years of empirical data to support their tools and techniques that can help decrease cortisol (stress hormone) and help increase DHEA (vitality hormone). I have been a certified trainer and coach for HeartMath for several years. These are great tools in my toolbox to help me to stay centered and calm. On my journey today, I am open to following what is placed on my path, and to trust my heart instead of being doubtful and afraid.

Again, why are people placed in our path? Maybe it is for you to learn from them, grow with them, help them, or perhaps they will help you. One day, a "random guy" at a shopping center asked me for money. I said, "I do not carry cash," and then added, "would you like me to buy you lunch?" He said, "*Yes, thank you.*" When we were standing in line, we had a conversation. He was a handsome, charming, 37-year-old guy who was having a hard time finding work. He shared with me that he had committed a felony at age 22 and had not been able to find a secure and steady job since that time.

We walked outside, and I started to do some research on my phone to find resources to help him find employment. At the time, I was heading to the library and asked him if he wanted a ride to the library. He got in the car and just sat. I noticed he did not have on his seatbelt. I asked him if he would please put on his seatbelt before we left. I wanted him to know that his life matters, too. He fastened his seatbelt.

It is sad that someone who made a huge mistake 15 years prior, when he was just 22 years of age, was still being penalized for it. How is this fair when some of the people who caused the fall of Lehman Brothers and Enron are not considered felons? Why does a 37-year-old man still have to pay for a youthful error that has not had the same expansive negative impact on our world like the actions of those at Enron did?

During my life, I have had the opportunity to travel around this vast planet. I have had the privilege of meeting some of the most amazing people, having awesome conversations and connections. An intention I set is to learn about others' perspectives, their thoughts, and why they think the way they do. While I may not agree with the things that they do, practice, or believe in, I am always respectful of them and their beliefs. They are human beings, and their opinion matters.

In my opinion, many of us are so wrapped up in our own world that we close ourselves off from the opportunity of meeting and understanding the people who surround us. Too many are overly busy keeping up with the Joneses. It is amazing to me to see how people value things so much more than connections with other human beings. Many people want a bigger car, a nicer home, a yacht, or a plane. Yes, these are all nice things; however, they can take away from your life if you cannot afford them. If that's the focus for happiness, it is time to reevaluate priorities.

On a lighter note, here is a funny serendipitous story. I was sitting at the bar in a restaurant, where my friend, Ryan, was the bartender. He turned and said, *"Cyrina."* Another woman at the bar looked up at that moment, we both said, "Yes?" Now you do not meet many Cyrina/Serenas. I reached out and said, "Is your name Serena/Cyrina too?" I was surprised because this had never happened to me before. The new Serena, her friend, Elizabeth, my friend, Jen, who was the GM of the restaurant, and I all began talking. We dove right into discussing some really inappropriate things! Luckily, the restaurant was closed at this time.

Serena and I have been friends ever since. As I write this, I am actually at Serena and her fiancé's home in Snowmass. I am watching their dog and looking at the beautiful view from their kitchen table. I like to refer to Serena as the *"Cool Serena,"* as I think she is much hipper than I am! If I had not taken the opportunity to talk to her that night, I would have missed out on being friends with an engaging personality and awesome person. It is interesting that: we wear the same size shoes and clothes; we each have been to Australia and New Zealand three times; and, unfortunately, we have both lost our fathers. Is this coincidence, or is it serendipity? I do believe we are supposed to be friends. Serena has been very supportive in my life, especially during the time of my accident. I am the sappy one, and she is the cool one. Sometimes, not often, we can pull the opposite side out of each other.

Interestingly, she has met an amazing Renaissance man, Glenn, and he rocks! Glenn is a talented artist, a professional fly fisherman, a contractor, a day trader, and a chef! WOW! He is just what she needs!

In this journey called life, you have to be open to the opportunities and connections that are right before your eyes! Unfortunately, many of us miss these opportunities, only because we are distracted by some unimportant detail. We are not present. We are fearful.

Now, a small world story, and the interesting events that occurred when I let my guard down. I had been in Europe by myself and was about to fly to meet a friend. I was sitting on the plane, while others were still boarding. A very attractive gentleman, who had an accent (that gives him 10 extra points right off the bat in my book) asked me, *"Is anyone sitting next to you?"* I said, "I do not know; they are still boarding." He said, *"Well, I am. I think you are beautiful, and I want to get to know you."* Alrighty then!

I put on my seatbelt and was ready for the ride. This scenario had never happened to me before, and I was excited to see what direction this flight would take. I thought, *Okay Cyrina, be in the moment and enjoy*! I wanted to emphasize this since women will often be thinking of what the future may hold and not enjoy the moment. He and I had an amazing conversation about life, the kind of impact one can have on our world, and the importance of continuing to expand and not to limit one's self.

My new flight friend, Liam, shared that he had been so focused on his business and reaching the goals he had set for himself, that he really had not dated in years. Now he was traveling to meet a woman, whom he had never met before, for a date...an international blind date. One thing led to another, and we started making out. Wow! I had never kissed anyone on a plane before this, nor since. Liam was an accomplished kisser, so I did not mind losing my plane kissing virginity to him. This unexpected, serendipitous flight illustrates how if you are open, the world can unfold. I am open to fun in the future, kissing on a flight, open to all the possibilities!

Even though he was on his way to meet a potential romantic interest, neither of us was in a relationship at that time, so game on! I got the feeling that maybe he wanted to freshen up on his kissing skills before meeting her. It was fun! We exchanged emails, and I wished him the best of luck on his blind date. I think we emailed maybe once shortly after, and that was the last communication we had had with each other.

Two years later, while I was searching through my emails for a webinar that I wanted to watch, an email from Liam suddenly appeared. I thought *you have got to be kidding*! It turned out that this webinar I signed up for was connected to his work. My random mile-high make-out buddy was employed by a business that hosted many of the webinars I had listened to in the past! WOW! I decided to reach out and email him, saying hello and asking how things had turned out on his blind date.

Funny enough, Liam shared with me that he had just proposed marriage to his international blind date less than a week prior. He was very kind in our communication via email; we both had nice things to say to each other. Liam said he was willing to help me out in the world of business, and he sent me a product that his company sells for $500 as a gift. The serendipity of that flight was amazing. I was single, he was single and honest. We had fun.

His international blind date had a great outcome. He obviously found his wife, and I was very happy for them. Excited for all the opportunities and possibilities that life presents to me. I am ready to go wherever life might lead me to experience great outcomes that align with my heart.

In my life, there are a whole host of serendipitous stories. I have shared these specific ones because I feel they demonstrate that no one really ever knows what is going to happen. If you are open to the possibilities, they can lead to new and exciting places. So, just lean in and see what evolves. We often put limitations on ourselves and situations. But things can change or shift on a dime, and therefore one needs to believe in the possibilities.

This thing called life is filled with so many exciting experiences! Feeling blessed, although I have also been challenged and tested quite a bit on this journey. With that said, I am ready for things to calm down a bit in my life! I have always been the responsible type; if I say I am going to do something, it generally gets done. I am also extremely honest and reliable. Until about five years ago, I would never have carried a balance on my credit card; however, now, things have shifted. It started when I began dating a very nice guy, with lots of children, expenses, and responsibilities. Financially, things were tight, although he seemed to move through with his resources on his credit cards and always paid for things.

We enjoyed our time together, although I was never in love, and neither was he. I will say that we had a lot of fun and great sexual chemistry! After 13 months of dating, this man decided to end the relationship via a text message. I was stunned! Was he 48 or 16 years old? This did not feel good. At first, I was shocked that he behaved so callously and secondly, I was sad. However, I then felt a great sense of relief that this part of his character had been revealed relatively early. I want to be with a man who would never choose to end a relationship in that manner. Therefore, I am thankful we are not together anymore. Recently, I found out that he had gotten married about 14 months after the end of our relationship, and is already divorced, which was another surprise for me.

I phoned him about a year and a half after the end of our relationship because I had continued to feel disappointed and hurt about how he had treated me. Sharing that I felt he had been very cold to have ended the relationship via text. Never before had I been treated with such disregard by someone I had shared a connection with for quite some time. He then shed some light on what had been occurring in his life, and the stress it had caused him. Even though I had no idea what he was experiencing, I still felt that his lack of communication had been unfair.

In my mind, everything happens for a reason. I am sharing this story because I would like to stress how important communication and treating others with respect is in our lives. Although my ex gets an F- in communication, I do think that he is a good guy. He caused me a lot of pain and hurt by treating me in such an inhumane way; I do not think anyone deserves such treatment. I challenge us all to put our best foot forward, even if it may be a harder step to take. Let's try to walk away from every relationship or situation, knowing we are leaving with grace.

With that said, the accumulation of debt, that I have never had prior in my life, is strange for me. I believe it is there to teach me the lesson that debt can happen to anyone! Thankfully my credit cards are at 0% interest; 0% interest is a great loan from a credit card. I will get the balances down before that changes. Although we may not be in control of the obstacles placed in our path, we are in control of the way that we handle them.

Takeaway Lessons from this Chapter:

* Challenges sometimes can slow you down and give you time to be reflective.

* Serendipity is a gift! Try to recognize it and then embrace it.

* Real connections that have been cultivated and grown over the years are well worth the time and effort.

* Kindness surrounds us if we allow it; quantum physics has illustrated the importance of the energy you feed the field.

* Never say never! You must be open to what unfolds in your life.

* The most conscious connection created in this chapter of my life was the serendipitous connection I had with Father Thomas Keating. His words, "Cyrina, it is all about love," have continued to resonate with my heart.

* What connections were created for you in Chapter 12?

Chapter 13

BIBS

BIBS (Brain Injury Benefit and Soiree) event on May 20, 2015, was a very memorable night for me. The event was the result of a mission to give back to two amazing resources that I had benefited from during my healing journey. Feeling so blessed for all of the support, comfort, and guidance I had received from Craig Hospital and RMHS (Rocky Mountain Human Services) during and after my stay in the hospital. I wanted to give back and arrange an event to raise funds for both of these places. The goal was to help other patients who were also dealing with head trauma.

It is funny how life works out. Wholeheartedly I believe you should be nice to people just to be nice, not because your kindness may benefit you. I became friends with Jen when she was 20 years old, seven years my junior. As there have been many Jens in my life, I gave them all different titles to distinguish between them, this Jen was "Baby Jen." 17 years later, this relationship made it possible for me to facilitate this amazing event. Now she has two children, and I can no longer call her "Baby Jen." You never know what life holds for you. With that said, I can guarantee kindness and happiness have positive impacts that resonate throughout the years.

Jen works for Big Red F, a local restaurant business. Over the years, I have developed positive relationships with many of her colleagues. One of them is Duane, an amazing chef and a hardcore snowboarder who had knocked his noggin a few too many times and was dealing with a brain injury as well. With this common link between us, Duane and I decided to work with each other to accomplish our mission: to help others with brain injuries.

Dave is the man who started Big Red F. At the time of the fundraiser, I had known him for about 17 years. He was so generous; he donated one of his restaurants, Jax in Glendale, Colorado, at no charge for the evening. The only thing we had to pay for was the actual cost of the food. Plus, all the employees and the eight chefs were very generous and donated their time. We also had plenty of liquor donated! The friendship with Jen has yielded many benefits and this one was 17 years after we had met.

Sara, at that time, was one of the managers at Jax. She was a rock star! She helped facilitate a smooth event with the amazing staff, delicious food, and an off-the-charts evening! I had never run a fundraiser before, but the recipients of the profits from the fundraiser, RMHS and Craig Hospital, were well-versed in this process. All of them, especially Annie and Erin from RMHS were instrumental in guiding us. Thank you, ladies!

Moreover, I had so many amazing friends who not only volunteered their time but also helped us with creative ideas, which yielded amazing donations for the auctions and sold tickets. Unfortunately, I am not able to mention all of the names of the wonderful people who helped this event be such a success! With that said, you know who you are and the amazing impact you had on this fundraiser. Thank you for your invaluable help!

This event took months to coordinate, but it was well worth all the time and effort. First of all, we were given so many compliments about the amazing staff, the delicious food and positive energy at the event. Many of the people who attended are huge philanthropists who go to fundraisers all the time. Therefore, I was floored to hear that BIBS had been one of the best fundraising events they had the pleasure to attend. I was so honored by this huge affirmation! I knew that we had been successful in our endeavors. The Jax staff provided superior service at the event; they donated not only their time but also all of their tips to the fundraiser. This, I feel, illustrated such a great message about the quality of people who made this event a huge success.

We had four speakers that evening. The first was Dr. Weintraub, my physician from Craig Hospital. He is an extremely well-known and sought after speaker which is no surprise, considering his vast knowledge and experience in the TBI world. He is not an inexpensive speaker, although he generously spoke and donated his time to the event. Though we did say, "Thank you for your time! We will buy you and your wife dinner."

I felt so blessed and excited that he had accepted our invitation, that he was available, and that he was willing to take us up on the exchange of his time for great food. I was appreciative that Craig Hospital had bought a table for eight people to support the event. Even Michael Fordyce, the CEO of Craig Hospital at that time, was there. I have found him to be such a wonderful and supportive person!

Another generous and eloquent speaker was Reverend Barry, who at that time, had been a preacher for many years. He had also experienced a head trauma, and his story is a powerful one. One night, he was driving and saw people who needed help. The kind man stopped to help these people. One thing led to another, and he was hit by a car while helping these people. He was struck in such a way that caused him to experience trauma to his head. We were so very fortunate to have had him sharing his story at the fundraiser. Reverend Barry's speech was captivating, inspiring, and moving.

Duane and I spoke as well. Three different people, who had varied types of head trauma and very different experiences spoke at the event. This was an illustration, in my mind, that you never know what people have experienced. I would like to digress here and state that everyone has a different story. We have all dealt with different obstacles in our life and many people have disabilities that are not visible to the eye. I do believe these experiences are lessons in our life, helping us grow and come to the realization that it is all about love. There are some very hard lessons in life. I feel we need to allow ourselves to try and bring our best selves forward. With this mentality, we can bring positive energy forward to help people with their struggles.

I was so nervous when it was my turn to speak in front of the crowd. I had to allow myself to breathe and be thankful for the amazing group of people supporting us! Many of my incredible friends, who I love dearly, were also present in the crowd, cheering me on. Despite my being so nervous, my speech flowed, and I felt surprisingly confident at being able to deliver my message so persuasively. I also received positive feedback about speaking in front of such a large group. I was very thankful to have that part of the evening accomplished. Then the time arrived for me to relax.

The decorations, the ambiance of the room, and the positive energy were really off the charts! The energy in the room felt magnified by the generosity of the amazing Jax team. The donation of their time, talent, and enthusiasm for one night had been a true act of charity on their part. We also had a band playing in between the speeches to optimize the mood of the room.

We had rented a large tent and set it up outside for the silent auction items. The tent also had an appetizer station, where people could have shucked oysters with all the toppings. I was so impressed by the number of generous donations we received from multiple friends of our BIBS fundraising group. Contributions from the Denver Broncos, the Colorado Rockies, alcohol distributors, artists, local spas, interior designers, and many more amazing gifts filled our tables!

At our live auction, we were fortunate to have been given unbelievable packages to bid on. Janelle Karas, a talented and professional auctioneer, with a generous soul, had donated her time and talent to our fundraiser. One of the packages that she auctioned off included a round of golf for four people at the Sanctuary, which is owned by Gail and Dave Liniger.

I have an interesting story about my connection to Gail and Dave Liniger. Dave had been a patient at Craig Hospital a few years after me. He was paralyzed; but thankfully, he had regained his ability to walk and decided to write a book: *My Next Step: An Extraordinary Journey of Healing and Hope*. He was speaking at a local bookstore and I was able to speak with him about his experiences at Craig Hospital. We were both thankful to have been at such an exceptional hospital whose staff had done its best to help us on our road to recovery.

When I arrived at the bookstore, I sat down next to a woman who seemed very friendly. I had no idea who she was. Being congenial, I struck up a conversation with her. I was surprised when I learned that she was Gail Liniger, Dave's wife. Gail had also been a patient at Craig Hospital many years prior, after a plane accident that she survived. Dave and Gail are extraordinarily generous individuals who have donated to Craig Hospital and also to BIBS. Specifically, they donated a round of golf for four people to play at their gorgeous private golf course, The Sanctuary. Friends of mine spent $2,200 during the live auction to win this prize. I was so thankful for their generous donation! Later, my friends stated that it had been the best round of golf they had ever played!

Other generous donations were made by my friends Diane and Christian, who have a beautiful property in Estes Park. They donated a bountiful package for a week at their cabin in the mountains. I have known Diane since the 10th grade in Florida, and now we both live in Colorado! She is the friend who made the beautiful, artistic, and inspiring Spirit box for me. We never knew whether or not our paths would cross again and I'm very thankful she is still part of my life.

Additionally, my old housemate Melissa's parents donated to the fundraiser. They own a beautiful B and B property with rustic cabins, called Cochran's Cabins on Saranac Lake, in New York. They also donated a generous package for a three-night stay at one of their cabins.

Friends I have known for 20 years, who live in Milan, Italy, have a wine exporting business. They, too, were generous, and the wine flowed because of them. Empson & Co. donated 48 bottles of a fantastic selection of wine to use for our silent auction. I was so excited that we had been able to generate such profit by auctioning our donations. I feel we did not just raise money, we also created awareness, formed connections, and initiated friendships.

I was so excited and thankful for the generosity of my friends, the owner of the restaurant, his staff, and the fabulous donations of people's time, energy, and auction items. We had been very fortunate to have had a hugely successful evening at the BIBS event. We had raised around $44,000 after our expenses were paid. I was blown away! I had never been so involved in co-hosting a fundraiser and was so pleased with the outcome. It had taken a surprising amount of work, although it was well worth the effort, energy, and time. In the world of fundraising, I was told this is considered a very successful first round for a fundraiser.

This experience opened my eyes to the intense amount of work required for preparing and hosting a fundraiser. Now, I have a new appreciation for all the efforts that go into fundraising events to make them successful. I am also now very appreciative of the importance of team effort and work. We had an amazing team of volunteers and employees to create the BIBS event and to take it to its shining success.

Thank you, Big Red F, Dave, the Jax crew, my amazing volunteer group, Sara, Erin, Annie, Janelle Karas, my friends, and all of the amazing people, for your time, donations and support.

Takeaway Lessons from this Chapter:

* Successful living takes a team effort!

* Being kind creates a ripple effect and the positivity may one day come back to you increased tenfold.

* We all have challenges in our lives. It is important to keep in mind that someone may be experiencing an invisible disability.

* Believing in and supporting your cause brings more attention and positive energy to the mission of your choice.

* We all have gifts that we can share to make a positive impact on our world.

* The most conscious connection created in this chapter of my life was the importance of giving back. The BIBS fundraiser not only raised money, but it also raised awareness of the invisible disabilities that might be present in other people's lives.

* What connections were created for you in Chapter 13?

Chapter 14

Learning through Connections

During the summer of 2017, I met a neurosurgeon from Iran who practiced in America. He shared an intriguing story with me that brought me to tears. He shared an account of a 17-year-old young man who was in a car accident with four other people. Everyone in the car died, except for the 17-year-old boy. He had suffered multiple severe injuries; specifically, he had a traumatic brain injury and things did not look good for him! The colleagues of this neurosurgeon thought that there was nothing more they could do to help the young man. But the neurosurgeon I met had a strong will and wanted to try to help this child to the best of his ability.

This physician was non-traditional in many aspects. His belief in the power of the mind was immense. This was something that he learned from his grandmother, and he had incorporated it into his personal and professional life. First, he had to identify the person this patient was closest to. As it was his sister, he had her visit her brother daily, spending most of the day with him. He asked her to touch her brother's arms, to tell him that he was recovering and that she loved him. She also collected many of his favorite songs; they had him wear headphones while she played the music he loved. When someone is in a coma, they are unaware of the time of day. The neurosurgeon prioritized keeping the young man on a Circadian rhythm; this positive stimulation occurred from 7 am till 10 pm.

This story reinforced what I knew to be true: a powerful and healing place to come from is love. When the neurosurgeon shared his story, I was touched and somewhat overwhelmed. My family had implemented many of these practices when I was in a coma. I can attest that love, positive stimulation, and empowering energy are what made a major impact on my healing process.

Neuroplasticity is a relatively new medical discovery helping us understand the complexity of the brain. It shows us the brilliance of this organ. It is neuroplasticity that allows the neurons in the brain to adjust their activity to compensate for an injury or a disease. This reorganization is aided by "axonal sprouting," the growth of new nerve endings from undamaged axons. They help reconnect the neurons whose links had been severed and stopped functioning. These new nerve endings sprout from the intact axons and help to create new neural pathways, and assume the functions of the damaged sections.

Brain-Derived Neurotrophic Factor (BDNF) is another major mediator in the plasticity of the brain. BDNF was apparently discovered in 1982; although I graduated from pharmacy school with my doctorate in 1994, I had never heard of this before my accident. BDNF helps facilitate synapse growth and supports the brain's function. It is a major player in the regulation of axonal growth and remodeling. Many things can affect BDNF. It is "activity-dependent," meaning we can affect its expression by performing certain activities. One of these activities is intermittent fasting, which involves going without food for 12-24 hours, which can increase BDNF levels.

I first heard of BDNF while reading a fantastic book I mentioned earlier, *Spark: The Revolutionary New Science of Exercise and the Brain*, written by John J Ratey, MD and Eric Hagerman. After my accident, a friend introduced me to this book. At that time, I wanted to learn how to optimize my brain health. Fortunately, before my accident, I was physically, mentally, and socially very active, which I believe, in my heart of hearts, was another reason I fared well after the accident.

Dr. Ratey speaks about exercise and how it is helpful with depression, anxiety, and ADHD. He shares this story about the importance of exercise and the production of BDNF. A very motivational teacher led physical education classes at a Naperville, IL high school. He helped implement zero-hour P.E., which was physical education before classes. This program is thought to be one of the primary reasons that this school excelled not just in fitness, but also in their cognitive abilities. The students placed in an international test called Trends in International Mathematics and Science Study (TIMSS). The students from this Naperville high school tested and ranked number one in science, just above Singapore and number six in mathematics in the world! This information alone should make physical education mandatory in school. Now there are even more reasons I need to increase my BDNF.

May 9, 2016, became a tough day for me. The effects of this day started to become apparent on May 10, 2016. On May 9th, I was working at the pharmacy. When it was time to close up the shop, I pulled down the gate and started cleaning up the day. I was putting away Genco Returns (drugs that cannot be resold). When I turned, a tote filled with drugs fell on my head. While it caused a little dizziness, I was very freaked out because of my previous injury. I began talking to myself, repeating over and over, *do not freak out, Cyrina, all will be okay*. I finished cleaning up, armed the pharmacy alarm system, and left.

I got home, trying to remain calm. I decided to allow myself to go to bed and sleep. The next morning, I woke up with a tremendous headache. I thought, *Shit, I better make a report about the injury*. This was the practical thing to do because one never knows.

Later that day, I received a message from a friend that her mom, one of my best friends, had passed away on May 10th. My dear friend, Mary Ellen, and I had been friends for over thirty years. She was the mother of two of my friends from Junior High, and I loved Mary Ellen.

She and Fred, her husband, had been married on the actual day of my birth, not just the day, but also the same year. We always called each other to celebrate 9/12. Mary Ellen and I connected on so many levels. Even though some years have elapsed since she passed, I think of her often. The year after, I texted her husband and two daughters, Maggie, who lives in India, and Molly in Florida, sending them my love. With this date being close to Mother's Day, I am sure it makes the entire experience and loss of their mother even more challenging.

On May 10, 2016, I had a broken heart with the loss of Mary Ellen, as well as a shooting nerve pain headache. I tried to stay calm. The headache continued, although I continued working while having pain. I was taking a lot of ibuprofen to make it through the day. A week later, I showed my housemate where I had placed a few things, yet I could not remember the word for a vase. I had to say, "You know, the thing you put the flowers in?" This memory challenge really freaked me out! We all forget words from time to time, but this was an elementary and common word. After this event, I decided to go to the ER that day. My worry had intensified. I couldn't convince myself to calm down this time.

Having memory issues is not an option for a pharmacist. Making a mistake can be life-threatening to others, and I am not willing to put my patients in danger. This had been an interesting year with many fears, questions, and procedures, as well as the daily pain in my head, tears, memory issues, and prayers. Thankfully, there was also growth and learning to have patience. I had to believe this was happening for a reason.

I was on a leave of absence from work while dealing with these memory issues and daily headaches. While visiting a store of the company I am on leave from, I met a colleague of mine. She is an extremely efficient and bright pharmacist, and she shared some upsetting words with me. She said to me that she had just put in her two weeks resignation notice. She was scared to work at this pharmacy, with all the changes resulting from the buyout of the pharmacy. She said she had left out four bottles of insulin (which must be refrigerated) because things are so incredibly hectic and stressful. They had cut her technician help by 35 hours a week, and she was being pulled all over the place. Another colleague told me it was like being in a pressure cooker in the pharmacy, and that she knew some other pharmacists that had to be placed on antidepressants or just quit their job. Having any memory issues in this "pressure cooker" environment was not an option. Talking to my colleagues elevated my stress and insecurity about working as a pharmacist. Even if the stress had not escalated, it could not be an option for me, as I did not want to bring any harm to anyone.

A pharmacist must have no memory issues! With that said, I am very disappointed that the company decided to cut the technician's hours. This is really not a safe model to implement. This is a formula for major issues and increasing the potential for errors in the future. Companies often only look at the bottom line, which is the almighty dollar. In doing so, they give up basic necessary needs which can be especially damaging when people's lives are potentially on the line.

Maybe the pain and the memory issues came for a reason. I think they were occurring because of a pinched nerve in my neck caused by the box falling on my head. This, in turn, caused the Ram's Horn nerve pain on the right side of my head. The pain in my neck travels over the right side of my head and my right eye. This has been an intense and interesting journey for me. Never had I experienced headaches that I can remember with the first accident. But I have had a headache daily for three and a half years, except for seven and a half days, after the tote fell on my head. I have decided I cannot let this pain steal my life. Still trying to live my life to the fullest, I feel robbed some days and do not succeed in doing so. With that said, I do have many things to be grateful for in my life.

Worker's compensation paid me for more than a year and a half and allowed me to see a nice, hip psychologist. While going through this process, I am aware that I may lose my career and identity. Therefore, this psychologist is helping me keep my mindset stable and positive. As I have been a pharmacist for 25 years, I know how big of a shift this will be in my life.

On many days, I think this journey is interesting. I know God has a plan! I am trying not to let fear take me over. With this ever-present pain I experience, I am burning up my neurotransmitters and seeing the emotional effects of it. I had been in a dark place a year after the injury at work. Usually, though, I am a happy-go-lucky, silly, and dorky person who laughs all the time. This has generally been the case in my life, except for the one month I mentioned earlier when I was so deficient in Vitamin D. This pain, the issues with my memory, and the over usage of my neurotransmitters because of the pain, had definitely made me feel depressed and questioning *why am I here*? I was placed on antidepressants for some time, and, thankfully, now I am not in that dark place anymore. With that said, I am still not back to where I want to be.

I never thought that I would have to be on antidepressants. This has been an eye-opening experience in many ways. For years, I have dispensed tons of antidepressants for my patients. I now have a clue about what depression feels like. I have been incorporating many other activities to help me deal with depression: saying my daily affirmations, exercising a ton, being outside in the sun and nature, getting and giving Big Hugs, connecting with my friends, and bringing more laughter to my life. All of these have had a very positive effect on me, my attitude, and my life.

Despite all that is occurring in my life, I will not allow myself to go down the dark Negative Nellie Road. I am trying to stay as optimistic as possible and notice what I am noticing, and not allowing myself to spiral down a dark path. This approach or attitude has always been a gift that came in handy at this point! While it has not been as easy for me to place myself in an optimistic place, thankfully, I have been able to admit that and ask for the necessary help! I am very appreciative to have seen the benefits of the antidepressants and to know that they helped me to climb over this hurdle successfully. I'm happy to report that I am psychologically doing well, having managed to taper off of the antidepressants. That said, I am conscious of my mood and am not afraid of going back on them if needed.

So many different modalities to help with the pain, including massage therapy, chiropractic work, physical therapy, acupuncture, drugs, and procedures have been tried. I had been very hopeful when going in for a procedure called a "medial branch block." They had injected a local anesthetic agent, either lidocaine or bupivacaine, into my neck, to decrease the pain. They did not tell me which agent they used, and unfortunately, there had been no improvement. Actually, after the procedure, there was additional nerve pain on the right side, plus intermittent pain that I experienced on the left side of my head. It seemed like the pain level on the right side had increased. This procedure does help some people, although it did not help me. It was not what I had expected and was, therefore, discouraging.

Now it was time to move on to other options. I remembered all the horror stories about worker's compensation doctors. Even though I, unfortunately, have not seen any improvement, I feel in my heart the doctors all sincerely want to help me. My case manager was a godsend. She was super helpful in getting procedures and care authorized, and she comforted me.

I am still experiencing memory issues and headaches, forcing me to reevaluate the direction of my life. Change is scary, although I have tried not to let my ego guide me. I am trying to allow my heart and soul to be my guide and to have light shine on my path. My light has dimmed since that box fell on my head and dealing with these daily headaches. After my severe bike accident, I returned to work within ten months. I have missed my patients, although bringing any potential harm to them was not an option for me. Now, I am attempting to realize my true path and hoping that this will all make sense one day. Even now, my heart is open to all possibilities, and I have not lost faith.

I just turned 49 and have never been married. Inviting romance into my life is on my list of what to focus on in my life. One day, the psychologist recommended that I get on one of those dating sites. He said the distraction might be good for me. I joked with him and said, "Do you think the worker's compensation will pay for the membership to Match.com?"

I delved into the world of different dating applications. It is an interesting world out there. After meeting a lot of guys, I have learned that if there is chemistry, then it is great. And if not, it still made for interesting stories! This process made me realize that some people in our world are not honest and some do not know how to communicate with others. Thankfully, I am lucky and have been blessed with the right skills on both counts.

I found one guy who was very attractive in his photo, and the feeling was mutual, or so he said. I was excited! We began to talk on the phone and texted each other daily. Even though we had not yet met, I was falling. He said he was out of town for work and that he might have to leave the country for a big project. He sent me his website and even sent photos of his flight tickets to Turkey, sharing with me his address in Denver. Things seemed legit, and I was getting excited and looking forward to meeting him when he returned. Thankfully, I then decided to do some slight stalking. I went by his "home," and saw it was for sale.

When we talked next, I told him, "I went to your home. It is beautiful, and it is for sale. Why are you selling your place?" He shared with me that after his wife had passed away about a year ago, he had felt like the house was too big for him alone and that he needed to start over. I believed him. This sounded like a legitimate reason. When I tried to FaceTime with him, he said his internet connection was bad. I told him, "Well, let's FaceTime when you have a good connection." But the FaceTime session never occurred.

He asked if the last company that contracted him could send his paycheck to me since he was out of the country. RED Flags shot up quickly. I said, "Let me think about this."

I felt very uneasy, so I called a friend of mine who is a police officer and asked if he could do a background check on this guy. He said he would have to open a case to do the background check. Trying to get creative led me to call the realtor of his "home" that was for sale. She shared with me that she had never heard his name before. That totally made me stop dead in my tracks and say, "Wow!" When I looked up his website again, it no longer existed.

If I had said yes to accepting his check, I would have been bamboozled. Thankfully, I was able to see that I was being lied to. Who knows what this guy was trying to accomplish? Whatever the intention was, it was based on lies. I feel sorry for humans who feel they need to manipulate and lie to achieve whatever outcomes they are looking to accomplish! I wasted a month of my time and had developed high hopes. Thankfully, we had not gotten involved enough for him to have his hands on any of my personal financial information. We have all heard stories about people who have been taken advantage of when they are only trying to find love.

The dating apps world is so interesting because of the myriad of experiences I have had and for the lessons I have learned. With that said, I also saw the dishonesty and miscommunication that runs rampant on such apps. I have met some great people on dating apps, but I have been shocked to see that some 50-year-old men on these sites still act as if they are in high school. Also, I am sure the same number of women who are superficial or have alternative motives are on these sites as well. I do not want to single out the male gender. A caveat to this statement, I most likely have zero idea about what is going on in a person's life. With that said, I want to be with a person who would allow themselves to be vulnerable and honest and see if there is a true connection!

We never think it will happen to us. I understand this, although it is extremely unfortunate to see the number of people without character in our world. Please be cautious out there and do not become victimized by these individuals with Zero, with a capital Z, integrity or good character!

I have several friends who were very successful using dating apps! I was actually a bridesmaid at the weddings of two friends who met their love on-line. Therefore, there is hope, and we have to put ourselves out there to find our partner.

My brother likes to say to me, *"Cyrina, everyone is f***ed up. You just need to find someone who is f***ed up the way you like it."* I believe this to be the truth! We all have our baggage that we carry with us. I encourage us all to realize that no one is perfect, including myself. However, I am still on the hunt for Mr. Right. I believe, without reservations, that he is right around the corner.

Takeaway Lessons from this Chapter:

❋ Life can throw you some curveballs, so get ready to dodge them.

❋ At times, there is no quick fix; you just have to put one foot in front of the other to move forward.

❋ If darkness arises in your life, please ask for help. Your life is important, and you need to see the light again. Please allow yourself to see a glimmer of light.

❋ When you are not psychologically well and experience depression, get help! Exercise, affirmations, sleep, laughter, connection, gratitude, counseling, and, if needed, antidepressants, can all help you move to the other side.

❋ Lack of integrity, unfortunately, is rampant in our world. Know you are worth more and do not allow yourself to become a victim.

❋ Life is an exciting journey as well as a gift. Let your positive energy and strengths shine, and help bring more light to this world!

❋ The most conscious connection created in this chapter of my life was to the power of the mind. Realizing the power of the mind has made me conscious of the mindset I set in my morning to propel me in the direction of my desires.

❋ What connections were created for you in Chapter 14?

Chapter 15

Catch Happiness

The October after the tote fell on my head brought all this uncertainty in my life. I used to lay in bed, praying, asking for direction, and guidance. One night, very frustrated, I said, "God, what the hell do you want me to do? Help me know what path I should be taking in my life." That night as I was lying there, all of a sudden, an idea flashed in my head. It made me hop out of bed and get on the internet.

I typed fast and felt extremely excited when the domain I wanted was available. This was the day I acquired CatchHappiness.com, for under $40. All that time, I kept thinking and feeling, "Wow, how is this possible?" This idea resonated in my heart and excited me, as I thought about the many different ways Catch Happiness® could help the world.

A few days after acquiring the domain, I was talking to a friend, a patent lawyer. I asked him how much it would cost for him to help me submit for a Trademark. He said, *"Cyrina, I am not going to charge you."* As you probably know, patent lawyers are not cheap, so this felt like another sign that this was the right direction or path to follow.

As a pharmacist for more than 25 years, I have seen people catch and spread many things! Now I want to encourage the world to catch happiness. Not only to catch happiness but also to spread it! I envision the day when pharmacists will dispense less medication to foster more prevention in a healthier and happier world. With that said, I am very thankful we do have medication to help people. Although with that said, our American society is overmedicated. I strive to see everyone achieve a better balance of their emotions. May we allow our thoughts to be more expansive and empowering, instead of constrictive and limiting.

Encourage a daily DOSE of Happiness. DOSE is an acronym: Dopamine, Oxytocin, Serotonin, and Endorphin. When I first saw this acronym, I remember thinking, "Wow, that is clever!". As a pharmacist, I especially love the fact that the neurotransmitters released during happiness fit the acronym DOSE. These neurotransmitters have positive effects on our physiology and can help us to create more renewing emotions. Life is too short not to be happy. I feel it has become my mission to encourage and facilitate people to enjoy this gift. Happiness is a choice we can make.

Currently, I am speaking to Meet-Up groups, schools, businesses, and hosting workshops about the positive effects of happiness, resiliency, vision as well as Conversational Intelligence®. These states of mind and techniques can facilitate productivity, creativity, as well as having a positive effect on an individuals' physical and mental health. I believe that we should encourage people to be happy NOW, not when they have accomplished x, y, or z in life. Remember, life is too short not to enjoy the ride!

No one person, institution, religion, business, or country has all the answers for humanity. We are all on this earth to grow and evolve into the best individuals we can be. We are on a path. Let it guide us to create the best families, businesses, communities, and world that we can. Unfortunately, life does not come with an instruction manual. We all have different ideas, motivators, and beliefs. Thankfully, as a female in America, I feel blessed to not only have an opinion but to be able to express it truthfully. While many people may not like what I have to say, I am allowed to be true to myself.

Shawn Achor is a brilliant guy who studied at Harvard and now has an inspiring company called Good Think Inc. He is sharing with the world the many outcomes of studies that he and his colleagues have conducted. By doing so, Achor is helping the world discover fascinating information about happiness. Achor and his colleagues have determined that when people are happy, it boosts our intelligence, creativity, and energy. Shawn Achor shares in his TED talk how very basic practices can help to elevate happiness and to help the brain to function more optimally. If interested, in watching Shawn, go to my resource page: to CatchHappiness.com/resources. It is very entertaining and educational. I encourage everyone to watch his TED talk. Many of the methods to help facilitate happiness that I shared with you: meditation, exercise, random acts of kindness, and gratitude, he shares in his TED talk.

In this book, we have talked about the importance of being in the moment. Shawn Achor speaks about the benefits seen by being in the moment. His work is a great resource for our world, and he is a hilarious guy as well! He has undoubtedly brought much insight and laughter to our world through his TED talk.

Gratitude is a practice by which we can shift our focus from the negativity in our world to the positive. Through gratitude, we can appreciate and celebrate the good things in our life that we often overlook due to the clouds of negativity and pessimism. As mentioned earlier, I encourage you to smile more often, to go out of your way to be nice to a stranger, give a sincere compliment, tell a joke, or practice whatever it is that brings happiness to you. If we implement these activities, they can allow us to shine. When you share these acts with the world, a chain reaction is created. Together, we can create gratitude in someone else's life and help other people Catch Happiness®.

As we are all different, we have various barometers for what brings happiness to us. So, to be part of the solution, let us help ourselves and our friends find our formula for happiness and actively contribute to the solution. The time spent will be well worth the return on investment.

I would like to suggest to all of you a book on kindness by David R. Hamilton Ph.D.: *The Five Side Effects of Kindness: This Book Will Make You Feel Better, Be Happier, Live Longer*. In the book, he speaks about the science behind kindness; it describes how the kindness molecules are released. Not all of us know this, but when we do an act of kindness, our system releases oxytocin and nitric oxide. These are what he calls the "Kindness molecules," and they are good for helping blood flow to the heart. Through kindness, you not only have the potential to help others catch happiness, thereby helping them increase their levels of positive neurotransmitters, but also to help yourself and your own physiology. In his TED talk, Dr. Hamilton shares the effects of kindness on our physiology. He says, *"If you live from the heart, it is good for the heart."*

If we take a moment to smile or say hello to someone, we will realize that these simple acts generate a positive impact on someone else's day, as well as ours! You never know what is going on in someone else's life. You have heard stories about people being nice to someone who was suicidal, and how that kindness resulted in that person changing their mind and deciding that they want to live. These acts of kindness do not take a ton of time, and they do not cost money. However, just being conscious of doing kind acts can be a challenge in our busy lives.

I feel the heart is where we need to come from in the world! Our hearts are such intelligent parts of our bodies. The science behind the heart and brain communication is off the charts! I would encourage everyone to look at HeartMath.com and HeartMath.org to see the amazing benefits their simple tools and techniques can bring into our lives. As I have mentioned before, I am a coach and a trainer for sharing their powerful tools that can help us to develop more resilience. These tools can be used while on the go, like when we start our day, when we feel agitated, and when we leave work. We do not need silence or darkness to implement these tools, although we do have to practice them to see the benefit. I have included just one section of information from their website that illustrates the positive outcomes from their tools and techniques:

"Studies conducted with over 11,500* people have shown improvements in mental & emotional well-being in just 6-9 weeks using HeartMath training and technology":

§ 24% improvement in the ability to focus

§ 30% improvement in sleep

§ 38% improvement in calmness

§ 46% drop in anxiety

§ 48% drop in fatigue

§ 56% drop in depression

Benefit statistics

* N= 11,903

"Percent of individuals often responding to always-on normed and validated pre and post Personal and Organizational Quality Assessment (POQA-R) (Reference: HeartMath.com website.)"

Life can get crazy busy, although by using the tools that HeartMath® shares, the practice can help to facilitate the outcomes listed above. Let us take the time to see what tools can help us on a daily basis to bring more flow to our day. It is worth the investment of our time!

My friend and graphic designer Dan Katai (Kataicreative.com) helped me create the logo for my business and the layout of the title on the cover of this book. Here is the logo.

*If you have the black and white version of this book, you can see the colors on the back cover. This will help with the visualization of the description of the logo.

The meaning behind the Catch Happiness logo starts with a smile that leads to a butterfly, reminding us to smile. Smiles can have a positive effect and generate renewing chemistry within our bodies! Plus, smiles are contagious, and this is something I would like to catch and spread. The butterfly equals metamorphosis or rebirth. It is made of two hearts: the right-side-up heart is in green and the upside-down heart in blue. The hearts illustrate the intelligence of the heart and that I am a Certified HeartMath® Trainer. The green color represents grounded, growth, and the heart chakra; the blue color is for the sky's the limit and the throat chakra.

Chakra may be a new word for many of you. Therefore, I want to share a basic idea of what it means. Chakra is a Sanskrit word that translates to a wheel or disk. The chakras are aligned with the spine and are wheels of energy that correspond with large nerve centers in our body. Our chakras may not be in flow and can cause secondary physiological, emotional, and mental, challenges. Allowing our chakras, a.k.a. energy centers, to be more in flow with energy can nurture vitality and the life force in our bodies.

Lastly, the dot of the 'i' is being carried away with the butterfly to represent "I am in flight." Dan and his talents, helped to create this simple yet meaningful logo.

We, hopefully, are always evolving and growing from what we learn in different areas of life. We sometimes need a reminder that we do have a choice. I want to create T-shirts, coffee mugs, stickers, and magnets with my logo on them to serve as reminders during our day to Catch Happiness®.

What energy do you want to feed the field? As we discussed earlier, we are all energy beings, and we can have an empowering or disempowering impact on our world. The decision is yours: what impact do you want to have on our world? You can always make money, but you can never make time. I want to encourage you to take advantage of your time and allow for expansion. Have a positive impact and help happiness to flow in our world! Do not wait to be happy anymore; embrace it in the moment.

I am looking into different ways to market these products and am learning about the many marketing modalities out there. This process is all new for me and I need to learn as much as possible. I went to a workshop on social media; the great business coach there gave me some strong advice, saying, "*Do not start with coffee mugs and T-shirts, write a book or start a blog.*" Hence, here I am.

I want to share with you a few stories that exemplify how I have been able to Catch Happiness® and share happiness. While standing in line at the grocery store, I noticed the shoes of a gentleman standing behind me; I thought they were cool and complimented him. We got into a fantastic conversation with lots of laughter. Although I may never see him again, we shared a very positive moment where we both caught happiness and laughter. Hence, I would like to put an idea out there: When we are standing alone in the line at the store, we can start up a conversation with the person next to us instead of surfing our phone. That is, if the person next to us is open to having a conversation. You may share laughter and a connection. This interaction may lead to the potential for many other positive outcomes. You never know!

I have made a concerted effort in my world to give sincere compliments to people who are older than I. We all know that as we age, the number of compliments we receive decreases. Although, I only compliment others if it is coming from a sincere place.

Many times, I will share a compliment with an older woman such as, "*Your hair looks very nice today.*" And a response I have received more than once was, "*Thank you. You do not know how much I needed to hear that today.*" I feel that a simple compliment had a magnified effect on this lady and was constructive. This moment made my heart feel good. I had no idea what was going on in her world, but I know that one minute of my time brought a moment of happiness to her. It also brought me happiness and a smile to both of our faces.

Smiles are part of the international language that we all speak. Traveling around the world has allowed me to realize that people, no matter where they are from, want to be happy. In America, we have so much material property, that I feel we have become so focused on things and not on people and potential experiences. On the other hand, I have been to foreign countries, where even when the people had very few material belongings, they were very wealthy in happiness. Music and sangria brought hours of fun and laughter.

I have always been a master at trusting my intuition. As a result, I have had a few moments that did not feel right, and my heart was feeling unsettled. When that happened, I decided to get out of the uncomfortable situation. I have to believe this all occurred for a reason. I love placing myself in a foreign environment and experiencing different cultures, thoughts, and ideas. I have traveled all around the world by myself. Although I live in Colorado, and I have not yet been to Wyoming; I often joke and say I have been to Vietnam, although I have not yet traveled to our border state of Wyoming.

Regardless of where I am in the world, I see similar types of personalities. Every culture has the confident, the insecure, the outgoing, the introverted, the silly, the serious, the laugh-out-loud, and the reserved. We may come from different cultures, but we are all humans who have the same basic needs. One of these common basic needs is love. Unfortunately, the current situation in our world is such that hate and separation seem to be pervasive in our world, especially in America. It has brought us to this place which has given birth to the Black Lives Matter Movement. I agree entirely with this statement, but I find it very sad that there is even a question of whether black lives matter or not! I personally believe ALL LIVES MATTER, regardless of what your race, ethnicity or what your beliefs are, everyone's life matters. I am not sure how anyone could think or believe differently. However, I do realize many people do not allow themselves to live from a place of love, and instead, they choose to live in a place of fear or hate.

While on a journey to Thailand many years ago, I was in a remote village. I had a digital camera when they were relatively new to the market. In this village, about ten children were playing, and I was taking their photos. I shared the photos on the camera screen with them, and they were so excited! It became evident they had never seen a digital camera before. They wanted me to take more photos, as they wanted to see themselves. Then, I had an epiphany and realized that they had never even seen themselves; they did not have mirrors.

Wow, this was such a wakeup call for me. This illustrated that they were all having fun together and it did not matter what they looked like! The way they looked had no impact on their ability to have a great time playing with each other. I saw them all smiling and having fun. Thankful to have had this experience, I felt joyful that they were playing and being children and not worried about how they looked.

It is sad that we take so much for granted in our lives. There are times when I wish we did not have mirrors. Unfortunately, in many scenarios, the exterior of a person means much more than who they are on the inside. Sadly, the inside of many people is not being nourished and optimized, although they may look amazing on the outside. I would like to encourage creating happiness on the inside and letting it shine through each person out into the world.

Takeaway Lessons from this Chapter:

❋ We can always reinvent ourselves. It may not be easy, but it is achievable.

❋ Catching and spreading happiness can help us all be more productive, creative, and have better physical and mental health.

❋ Logos may look simple, although they can be layered with tremendous amounts of thought and meaning.

❋ Kindness can be good for the heart.

❋ Shawn Achor's TED talk brings laughter and insight.

❋ HeartMath* is an invaluable resource.

❋ Remember, a smile is a part of the international language.

❋ The most conscious connection created in this chapter of my life was the impact of happiness. The clear science behind the benefits of experiencing happiness reaffirms my desire to help people Catch Happiness.

❋ What connections were created for you in Chapter 15?

Chapter 16

Alternative Healing Modalities

We live in such a busy, fast-paced, crazy, and wound up world that being able to sit and meditate for a moment may seem impossible at times. However, meditation can help clear that constant chatter and stimulation all around us, as well as quiet our inside minds. Different kinds of meditation have helped with multiple health challenges. This is not a hoax; this is the boundless power of the mind! I believe that there is a responsibility to educate and teach everyone the tool of meditation to help us develop a sense of being centered in our lives.

I highly recommend a fantastic book written by Dr. Norman E. Rosenthal MD, *SUPER MIND – How to Boost Performance and Live a Richer and Happier Life through Transcendental Meditation*. Dr. Rosenthal shares with us many of the amazing benefits and the positive outcomes of meditation. He shares stories of highly successful people who incorporate meditation into their daily lives. One of these is Ray Dalio, the founder of Bridgewater Associates, which is one of the world's most prominent hedge funds. He is a very successful and, I am sure, an extremely busy man, but he meditates twice a day every day. This time allows him to be more focused and productive and allows time for important answers to be revealed.

Ultimately, is meditation for everyone? Each individual would have to determine this for themselves. I have participated in group contemplative prayer/meditation, and I can verify that the positive energy created is out of this world and almost tangible! It is fascinating to feel the positivity in the room during the practice. It is not something you can master overnight; it is a practice. That said, I do believe that this free resource must be encouraged and taught, especially to our youth. It can help them feel more in flow and self-regulate with increased focus. People, especially patients in a hospital setting, are dealing with challenges, and meditation can help to bring some calmness to their days. Meditation alone, or augmented with standard treatments, can have a multitude of benefits.

Exposure to positive energy is known to fuel and contribute to desired outcomes. I have not conducted a study on this, but generally, when someone is positive, they attract more positive energy, and the same goes for negativity. What do you like to surround yourself with? We now know that in general, we adopt the habits of the people we spend the most time with. Jim Rohn said it well: *"We are the average of the five people we spend the most time with."* Hence, who we surround ourselves with has a direct impact on us. We may want to be more selective about our choices. We are all energy beings. We have to make decisions about what energy we want to send out, surround ourselves with, and attract.

Our brains can be all over the place and unproductive. In this state, our minds can take us to not-so-pleasant places, and as a result, we are not efficient with our time. Our time is one of our most precious assets. You can always make money, although you can never make time! Fulton Oursler's quote, *"Many of us crucify ourselves between two thieves - regret for the past and fear of the future"* is thought-provoking. His quote inspired the rewording of the statement I mentioned earlier:

Sadness and regret are the past;

Fear is the future;

The moment is a present.

We can agree that the moment is not the easiest place to arrive. However, I will say it is well worth the practice to stay in the present. The practice of meditation or mindfulness can help us be present.

Many different resources are available that can help us become more centered. We can choose to practice meditation, yoga, music, exercise, giving a hug, or whatever else helps us feel present. We can choose a personal activity to aid us to become centered. Soon, after continuous daily practice, we will understand how being centered on our path is such a huge gift. When we are present, calm, and centered, we can mimic a school of fish. This is the feeling of being in the flow, more productive, and optimizing our energy expenditure. When this activity is put into practice, we are allowing ourselves to shine. Shawn Achor states, *"When we are happy - when our mindset and mood are positive - we are smarter, more motivated, and thus more successful. Happiness is the center, and success revolves around it."* Achor also shares, in his TED talk, that research shows that the neurotransmitter dopamine is released when we are happy. Dopamine is powerful - it turns on ALL the learning centers in the brain. I think it would be fascinating to laugh and smile as much as possible in our mornings to see the positive effects these behaviors have on our ability to think and learn.

When listening to the book, *Outwitting the Devil,* written by Napoleon Hill, many concepts emerged. Hill was such an amazing author with incredible insight. Through many of his books, Hill helped his readers know that the thoughts we allow to run wild in our minds can create empowered outcomes or our own hell on earth. When I was talking to Thomas Keating (the Catholic monk and priest), he also shared the idea that many people create their own hell on earth.

I had not given much thought to the words that Thomas shared until this time in my life. Today, I feel like I am in the flow, although I am dealing with many challenges. This means feeling that I am in the current of life, and I am not going to fight it by trying to swim upstream. Although, there are many uncertainties and some fears in my life now. I think that there are signs placed on my path to help me recognize that I am in flow and on the right path.

The thoughts that we allow to play through our heads are soundtracks with the capability of making us believe many negative, untrue things about ourselves. We all have memories of soundtracks from movies or TV shows, which transport us back to places in our past. These recollections can be filled with positive memories, laughter, inspiration, and can be constructive for us. On the other hand, they can also carry us to places of fear, upset, insecurity, and disempowerment. It is impactful how listening to only a few seconds of a soundtrack is so powerful that these links start to form.

The same is true of the emotional soundtrack of our lives. What did you hear people say to you when you were a child? What is the nature of the people you surround yourself with today? Do these individuals complain about or criticize people in general? Or do they embrace others for their strengths? Frequently, I am surprised by the impact of this simple awareness; we can choose what to have in our daily lives and in our belief system.

There are perceptions and editors who like to come in and change our daily soundtrack; I refer to them as the "Soundtrack Gremlins." They edit in phrases or thoughts that are not empowering, internal dialogue such as: "You are not good enough!" "Are you kidding, you will never accomplish that." "You are not pretty enough, or you are not handsome enough," and "They do not like you." The list is never-ending. Have you ever heard such soundtracks playing in your head? The question is how do we stop the "Soundtrack Gremlin" editors from causing such a negative impact on our mindsets?

WE are able to tell these Soundtrack Gremlins to stop with the negative chatter. We must also realize that we do not need the Negative Nellie or Ned editor in our lives. HeartMath® introduced me to the idea of the emotional soundtracks, they also have helpful resources to shift our depleting emotions.

Another amazing book and resource is *Solve for Happy* by Mo Gawdat, who was the Chief Business Officer for Google X. He shares his journey and the loss of his son, Ali. His book gives so many examples of how each of us chooses to look at and live our life.

While having a Zoom® conversation with Mo Gawdat, I told him I loved *Solve for Happy*, particularly the story of Tim and Tom. I feel they are excellent illustrations of the Soundtrack Gremlins. In his book, one morning Tim and Tom face similar situations; however, they handle the events very differently. One has a positive outlook toward a potentially challenging morning, while the other tackles the challenging day with a negative outlook. It is fascinating to observe how the outcomes are the direct result of their differing mental posture.

In our daily experience, perceptions can have a vigorous empowering or disempowering impact on our lives. Gawdat, a very bright man, shares in one of his chapters a complex mathematical illustration to prove there is a God! I was so thankful he included this in his book, along with other enlightening thoughts and stories. I highly encourage everyone to read this insightful book, *Solve for Happy* by Mo Gawdat.

Allowing positive affirmations into our lives can help decrease the potential takeover by the negative Soundtrack Gremlins and help us shine. Also, I feel so honored to have been exposed to the wonderful teachings of Louise Hay, author of *You Can Heal Your Life* and many other books. One of her famous positive affirmations, *"Life loves me,"* is so very true! Louise Hay, a light in our world, has shared so much about how our thoughts impact our health.

Many of you may be familiar with Louise Hay or with Hay House Inc., her publishing company. Having such an inspirational story, she has written many books about love and how powerful love is to heal oneself. She has helped our world become a better place. If you have not heard of her, I highly encourage you to Google her name and introduce yourselves to an amazing woman who was an author, speaker, healer, artist, and a clear illustration of an amazing human. She was such a conduit to love as well as forgiveness.

I feel honored to have been able to attend her 90th birthday celebration. *"You Can Heal Your Life",* named after the book that Louise Hay wrote, was the title of her celebration. Anyone could attend after paying $90; all of the proceeds were donated. The celebration was in San Diego at the convention center. Some inspiring speakers were invited to present at the event, all of them are authors who themselves have made a significant impact on our world. These speakers included: Cheryl

Richardson, Christiane Northrup MD, Mike Dooley, Kris Carr, Robert Holden, and Suze Orman. All of them brought different elements to the day by sharing their inspiring and entertaining stories, as well as parts of their journeys. They also shared stories about the positive impact Louise Hay had on their lives.

The energy and love in that arena were unbelievable! I was super excited to have taken that journey to celebrate her life. Louise Hay had faced many very challenging experiences during her life with love and forgiveness. I believe this is why she had such a positive impact on our world. So many recognized teachers and leaders have been influenced by Louise Hay and her amazing path and teachings of positive affirmations.

On Thursday, August 31, 2017, I woke up to the disheartening news that an angel in our world, Louise Hay, had left the earth the day before, on the 30th. She was an extraordinary woman who will live in my heart forever. I was so grateful to have been present at the celebration of her 90th birthday. A memorable teacher, she left us with so many gifts. Thank you, Louise Hay.

We all have to learn to evolve and grow into our lives and our purposes. If we keep our eyes open and ready to see, our teachers will appear. I try to be conscious and in flow with my life. I never want to become stagnant; always wanting to learn, grow, and become a better person. I strongly believe that specific people are placed in our lives to help with this process. Many offer guidance, friendship, and love, while others may introduce us to frustration, anger, or fear. We all make mistakes. With that said, there is a spectrum of potential errors; no one is perfect! If we can lead our lives with love, forgiveness and without judgment, as Louise Hay did in her life, our world will be a much more peaceful and harmonious place.

So much literature identifies stress as the major culprit behind the negative manifestations that occur in our bodies. It is also interesting how an individual's perception of stress can affect how they respond to frustration, conflict, and challenges. Shawn Achor shares with us: *"If we can move stress in our life from a threat to a challenge, it turns out it transforms the effects upon you."*

All of us must find for ourselves a method for stress release. This will assist us in moving through stress more successfully during our lives because, unfortunately, stress will present itself. Whether we adopt meditation, cardio exercise, attend a dance party, use a punching bag, or practice yoga, we can empower ourselves if we find a stress release mechanism that works for us. Holding on to stress is never the optimal thing for our physiology. The effects of stress can increase heart rate, headaches, muscle tension or pain, fatigue, stomach upset, and difficulty sleeping, to name a few.

Because those gremlins in our soundtrack can always induce stress, what mindset will you allow and establish? How does that soundtrack play out, and what manifestations does it have on you, your body, your relationships, and your life? These are questions that we all can be motivated to find our personal answers to. Many times, our soundtracks are destructive because we do not communicate clearly and openly with our friends, family members, or colleagues. Unfortunately, there is not a class in high school that teaches us the basics of communication to create more effective, positive relationships in life.

It is fascinating to me how much we are learning about our bodies, the chemicals that are released, and our intelligent system. We now know that oxytocin or cortisol are released during different types of conversations; these can and do have specific effects on our physiology and the use of our prefrontal cortex. I just became certified in Conversational Intelligence®. The neuroscience behind conversations can have a significant impact on our brains. Our prefrontal cortex region of the brain is activated by oxytocin. It is the executive functioning area of the brain that facilitates making more logical decisions. When we are feeling threatened in our conversations, we release cortisol, and this decreases blood flow to our prefrontal cortex. How can we optimize our thoughts, conversations, and actions to have an impactful effect rather than an impairing one on our physiology?

In 1942 the term Epigenetics was introduced by Conrad H. Waddington. Waddington, who was a brilliant British developmental biologist, geneticist, embryologist, paleontologist, and philosopher, who laid the foundation for many things, including Epigenetics. He was granted many awards from various highly regarded British Societies for all that he brought to the world of science. Epigenetics brings a whole new approach to health and living by explaining the impact of different things in our environment. The environment can impact the expression of an individual's genes and overall health. We have long thought that the DNA we were dealt was our destiny. For many years, we have believed that we had little control over our genetics, which determined much of the outcome of our lives through our health, our body, and our personalities. Yes, we are all inherently born with DNA, and it does have an impact. However, we now know we are more in control than we previously thought, and that we are capable of making shifts in our gene expression if we choose.

Now we know that regardless of the genes we are born with, some may be turned on or turned off. What controls the on and off switch? This is where Epigenetics plays a major role. A few impactful environmental elements include: What do we eat? What environment do we live in? What friends or people do we associate with? What type of interactions do we have with people? When and how much do we sleep? Do we exercise? Do we have an outlet to release stress? What soundtracks are playing in our minds? Are we allowing the gremlins to be at work? Is our director Negative Nellie/Ned or Positive Polly/Paul? We must become conscious of this and have the confidence and insight to make the necessary shifts.

I want to draw an illustration, adapted from an article in WhatisEpigenetics.com, entitled *"A Super Brief and Basic Explanation of Epigenetics for Total Beginners."* Hopefully, this story will shed light on the role of Epigenetics on our physiology. Let's imagine that your life is a long epic movie. The actors and actresses of this movie are the cells in your body. Since your cells are constantly reproducing, you can always change the actors and actresses. Your DNA is the movie script that the cells must follow, while the sequencing of the DNA are the words in the script. Specific blocks of words from the DNA instruct key actions to occur; these are the genes. Screenwriting conceptually plays the role of our genetics. Epigenetics has a very important role as the director, who can alter the script by adding or deleting certain scenes, changing the dialog, or creating a movie that has a very different feel. The group of words can be associated with our genes. Therefore, the original script has remained the same, although the director's decisions to add or delete certain sections of the script, analogous to our genes, have changed the completed work. You are the director of your life. What outcome do you want for the movie called, "Your Life?"

Ava DuVernay is an accomplished and talented director known for her movies: *"A Wrinkle in Time," "Selma," and "13th,"* to name a few. I had the lovely opportunity of meeting her after hearing her speak at the Ideas Festival. She is giving aspiring directors the opportunity to shine and share their talent. Ava DuVernay has shown the world that you can succeed regardless of your circumstances! When speaking, she stated something along the lines of our DNA is being affected by our environment and by the words said to us. Her description reminded me of Epigenetics, and we had a lovely interaction about the truth of her statement after her talk. She is helping the world to write a better movie and encouraging us all to be good humans, and to share our gifts - we all have one. If we had a creative director such as Ava DuVernay, the expression of our genes would be magical and allow us to be our best!

I am encouraging us all to take inventory of our life's elements, as well as who we want to be in our life! This is a process that begins with the questions:

※ How can we be our best?

※ How can we surround ourselves with the most positive influences to be the leading roles in our movie?

※ To shine and create our award-winning movie, a.k.a. our life, let's all help each other to take notice of the energy we are bringing to our surroundings and allow ourselves to level up!

※ Let us be conscious of the things we say to others as well as ourselves. Are the statements we use empowering and expansive or disempowering and contractive?

May these questions help you live a life you love!

Takeaway Lessons from this Chapter:

※ Meditation is a fantastic vehicle that can help us be more present.

※ There are many amazing resources available for free at the library. Books are a great gift that can help all of us grow and evolve.

※ Mo Gawdat's outlook and insights are enlightening in *Solve for Happy*.

※ Louise Hay was a gift to our world. By sharing her life and insights, she helped us to see the importance of love and forgiveness.

※ Ava DuVernay is a magical director; may we all learn from her.

※ Epigenetics is a game-changer.

※ The most conscious connection created in this chapter of my life was connecting with Louise Hay. This has been such an important gift in my life for all the impactful teachers placed on my path by Hay House Inc.

※ What connections were created for you in Chapter 16?

Chapter 17

Finding your Match

Do you remember the story I shared about Tim and Tom from the book *Solve for Happy*? I feel there are some parallels between that story and a personal event I am going to share with you now. It is a perfect illustration of how people perceive the same situations differently. When two people experience extremely similar events in life, the outcomes can be completely different. The primary reason for the dichotomy in the outcomes is the different attitudes and perceptions of the two people. To better explain it, let me paint a picture.

This event happened to me while I was in the process of writing this book. So I thought I would share it to give you an even deeper look into my reality. At the time, I was on multiple dating apps - oh the world of dating! I have found the process of dating apps very interesting; not only that, I have met some very intriguing people through the process. Join me on this journey as I share what occurred one night.

The first time I meet someone is not a date in my mind, I schedule an initial meeting, simply to see if there is any chemistry between us. The meeting is usually just one hour long, and if there is chemistry, then we will schedule a date for the near future.

For this particular meeting, I invested quite a bit of my personal time getting ready. I curled my hair and spent time on my makeup; then I drove forty minutes. The meeting place was a halfway distance location for both of us.

When I arrived and saw that he wasn't there yet, I texted him. He responded and said he was still in surgery; unfortunately, he was not able to meet me. He was an oral surgeon, a nice and busy man, though he lacked consideration; he was not proactive when it came time to cancel our meeting.

We had miscommunicated. Obviously, unplanned and unforeseen things come up in life. At that moment, his patient definitely needed him more than I did. I decided to have dinner on my own. I sat down by myself at the bar and ordered a drink. This handsome young man came up to me and asked me if he could sit next to me. He was visually appealing and seemed nice and of legal age, although he was 19 years my junior.

He and I had an interesting, in-depth conversation, and I was intrigued. I decided to order food, and he told the bartender to put it on his bill. Taken aback, I told him, thank you but you do not have to pay for my dinner. In response, he complimented me and said he wanted to pay. I just thought to myself, *wow, this is so nice of him!* We ended up spending a few hours together, just talking and enjoying each other's company. I was very flattered to have a 28-year-old man, be so present and off-the-charts nice to me.

Now, I know that this is not the kind of meeting that happens every day. I was very impressed with him and enjoyed our time together! I did not expect someone of his age to be detached from his phone and stay so engaged in a meaningful conversation! He was a wonderful, attractive, interesting, and generous guy. Though things had not gone as planned with the oral surgeon, I still had an enjoyable evening.

The "random" nice guy and I said goodbye to each other. I walked around the outdoor shopping area and ran into a colleague I had not seen in over a year. She was there with her husband and her two adorable grandsons. With this small group, I shared my ideas about my desire to talk to students about the science behind Epigenetics, creating more happiness in our world, and the energy in our environment.

They had some great feedback and enthusiastically added, "You should speak at our school!" My friend said she would help facilitate my ideas. While it was amazing to run into her, I felt so fortunate to have met her husband and two of her grandchildren. I never know what "random" meetings will blossom into. She and I had a lovely conversation, and we decided to get something on the calendar and connect soon.

After I spent my time and energy getting ready, driving 40 minutes, and the oral surgeon did not show up, I could have allowed myself to be frustrated and pissed. But I didn't. Thankfully, I ended up having an evening filled with a very positive and an unpredictable sequence of events. If I had not been stood up by the oral surgeon, I would have missed all these incredible interactions! Plus, one never knows where any interaction or meeting might lead. This is one of the main reasons I want to encourage each of us to allow ourselves to be present in the moment and to be optimistic. Negative Ned and Nelly attract negative events into their lives. Positive Paul and Polly look for the unfailing, and allow good things to flow into their lives, even if a black cloud temporarily covers them.

We are all trying to figure out this thing called "life." It is like a science experiment where we can make a hypothesis by trusting our intuition. Many times we are right, and other times there are surprises in store for us. Sometimes, the data just does not correlate. I encourage people to put this common word, "communication," into practice. It is so interesting to see how an individual ignores a situation that often stops others from responding and explaining their thoughts and actions. Sometimes, people just do not want to listen to others. They are happy to believe the flawed assumption that they can read other people's minds. Communication is key to cultivating true relationships with a strong foundation!

I am very fascinated by how people find their life partners. Serendipity, at times, can blossom in very unlikely ways. Let me share with you an illustration of what I mean. This is the story of how two of my friends found each other (hint: it was not on a dating site). This story exemplifies how something positive can blossom out of negative events. Sometimes I call these tales the silver lining that appears within life's adverse circumstances. You have to be open to allow your resilience and light to shine through the dark days. I encourage you to buckle up because you are about to take a very interesting ride!

It was wintertime a few years ago, and my friend Kate and I had gone skiing with mutual friends. We had stayed in the mountains and really enjoyed our time together, which was filled with lots of laughs and great skiing. During this visit, Kate mentioned to us that she was going out of town and needed someone to watch her dogs. I, unfortunately, was not available to help her out. Our married friends, Donald and Susie, said, *"Oh, our daughter loves dogs and would be happy to take care of your home and your dogs."* Now, we had never met their daughters, although we had known Donald and Susie for years and thought the world of them. Kate was relieved because she was leaving the following weekend.

Kate decided to hire their daughter, Jackie, who was in her mid-twenties at that time. Kate left a bouquet of flowers, a bottle of wine, as well as money for Jackie. Kate was going to be away for four nights and five days. On the second night of Kate's vacation, she received a phone call from AMEX asking if she had authorized a $1500 charge to Best Buy. Yikes, she had not! She was obviously very alarmed. She ended her vacation with her parents early and got on a plane home. Meanwhile, she contacted a mutual friend of ours to go over to her home to relieve Jackie and to take care of her dogs.

Kate returned to find that a nightmare had taken place in her home. It turned out that Jackie, with her lack of character, was not exactly a person Kate or anyone else would want in their home. We were both so incredibly shocked by the fact that people who we really liked and trusted had a daughter like Jackie. We also couldn't believe that Donald and Susie had even contemplated, let alone arranged, the horrible nightmare that their daughter created for Kate. For support, I went over and stayed the night with Kate until her parents arrived.

It was the start of an extremely time-consuming and stressful process for Kate. The locks on all of her doors had to be changed. It turned out that Jackie was a methamphetamine addict and had invited some of her drug buddies into Kate's home. (This is not what you would have expected from friends who you trust, who had referred their own daughter.) Jackie and her drug buddies stole Kate's identity and charged many things on her credit cards. They also used Western Union to access her money. As Kate is a physician, they compromised her computer and got access to her DEA number. They created a big mess that Kate, on a daily basis, found more horrible things that they had done.

I was shocked that Donald and Susie had recommended their daughter to house and dog sit for Kate. I have to believe that they had some idea that their daughter was struggling with challenges. They were non-apologetic and did not offer to help with cleaning up the mess their daughter and their referral had created. I was so disappointed by their total lack of character and concern for Kate. Although Susie and Donald are extremely wealthy, they lack the core ingredient of a good character that is called integrity! Their behavior was totally unexpected, and it was difficult for me to believe this event occurred.

As I mentioned before, there is a silver lining with the most challenging situations. Kate's parents had arrived, and things continued to unfold. The policemen, working closely on the case, tried to find out about the drug buddies who had been invited into Kate's home by Jackie. The men who had stolen Kate's personal information were well-seasoned in this type of activity. During the investigation, we learned that one of them had already been incarcerated for a similar crime. This was a mentally, emotionally, financially, and physically draining situation.

One of the police officers was extremely nice to Kate. Just a side note: Kate is beautiful inside and out, and she is also very successful and intelligent. She has a beautiful heart. The police officer, Dylan, really took a liking to her. At this time in her life, Kate was very vulnerable. This event was not a common occurrence for her. As time went on, Dylan and Kate kept the relationship strictly professional with a bit of flirting taking place. If Kate and Dylan had met at a single's bar, I do not think Kate would have even entertained a potential romantic connection with him. I state this for several reasons: he was nine years her junior and has a sleeve of tattoos! Dylan would not have met Kate's criteria for a mate from her past list of must-haves.

However, I started to notice a few little signs, which made me very curious about what was happening in Kate's world. Kate's vulnerable state allowed her to let down her barriers, to open her heart, and to accept love from a nontraditional person. I was so amazed and impressed with this sequence of events! While Dylan does not hold a graduate-level degree like Kate, he is extremely intelligent and attractive. He is also an amazing cook, a skill set that Kate has very scant knowledge of.

While she was falling for Dylan, he had already arrived! Before I knew it, Kate and Dylan were dating. I was so proud of Kate for allowing love into her life from the most unexpected initial meeting and circumstances. The turn of events is so fascinating because the two of them likely would have never met if the nightmare of identity theft had not happened in Kate's life.

Kate and Dylan dated for a short time; then, he proposed. I was so excited and surprised how quickly all of this had unfolded. Moreover, it was an exciting honor to have been asked to officiate their wedding! In Colorado, the laws are a little vague about who can perform marriages, so I have been able to add this notable role to my resume. I spent the required $19.95 to become Reverend Cyrina Bullard, granted by the Universal Life Church. In my opinion, it is the best money I have ever spent online to date.

Kate and Dylan make an admirable couple! I am very excited for them and their future. Their families get along so well, and they love each other's parents and siblings. Their story is thought-provoking and just reconfirms for me that the journey of life is so interesting. You never know what your day might hold.

I have found that being flexible and allowing my day to unfold the way it does, without forcing things, helps to decrease anxiety in my life. Obviously, there are limits to this relaxed approach, since we do have to accomplish many tasks during our day. However, instead of getting frazzled and upset when things do not go exactly the way we have planned, I believe that this is a time to let go because sometimes the unexpected shift leads to something amazing! We are all different and need to find and implement the tools that help us to enjoy our journey.

There have been times when I was frustrated because I was running late. Finally, when I got on the road, there was a severe car accident that had just happened. These situations make me think, "Did running behind schedule save my life?" "What matters more, Cyrina, that I was late or that I arrived alive?" This train of thought obviously made me very thankful that I had been running late.

Daily living has many potential outcomes. Yes, I have had a lot of challenges in my life although I have had even more blessings. That said, I would like to challenge everyone (including myself) to grant yourselves three days filled with positive thoughts and NO complaining. You will be able to appreciate the small and wonderful gifts in your world during this time. I am interested to know what shifts will occur during these days.

Let's start slow. Just try one day and see what your overall feelings and outcomes from the day are. Was the outcome worth not having a bitchfest in your day? Then you can incorporate these three-day challenges into your lives at least once a month, nothing too extreme. There are obviously no guarantees, although there are no side effects to being positive and not complaining. May all of us have good luck with our three-day personal science experiment. Let's see how things unfold and what findings we can discover.

As with any new endeavor, it is helpful for us to have support, a partner in crime, for encouragement. You can choose a family member, a friend, or a person who is in your daily life. Be present and try this experiment together. Select a person to be a positive thoughts and no complaints buddy who will be an accountability partner. If you start to complain, and even if it is legitimate, you cannot be allowed to continue. If you continue to complain, then your 72-hour experiment has to start over. This will, at times, not be easy, although I can tell you that it is well worth the effort. Having a bitchfest every once in a while is not a bad idea because everyone has to release frustration, and it can be therapeutic. However, let's allow a change in the frequency we release, by switching from the "bitchfest station" to the "having gratitude station." Allowing yourself a 30-minute window to release frustration and hit the reset button, is a great gift.

Back to my bicycle accident. I realized that I needed to experience the feeling of gratitude for even the smallest things, such as going to the bathroom alone. Unfortunately, I feel that we, as a society, are always looking for bigger and better things.

I encourage you to allow yourself to love experiences more than things. Some examples include: going on a beautiful hike with your friends or family, watching a silly movie, bringing a smile or laughter to a colleague. All of these are positive experiences that bring joy to your life.

You can have that ripple effect and the blossoming of magical memories! While you experience these positive moments, try to be as present as possible. Instead of having a house filled with possessions, focus on making your life experiences and relationships more beautiful and expansive.

Takeaway Lessons from this Chapter:

❋ Your attitude towards a situation can have a positive or negative impact on you, your life, and others.

❋ Do not get all worked up over things that do not unfold as you have planned.

❋ There are silver linings found in many unfortunate situations.

❋ Allow yourself to be open to opportunities you may not have seen before.

❋ Writing down our gratitude has a positive impact on us, as well as on our world.

❋ Allow yourself to take a complaining break. Be conscious and capable and see how your day unfolds.

❋ The most conscious connection created in this chapter of my life was the connection with Dylan. In my mind, Dylan illustrates that amazing people can be introduced to you during the most challenging times. Regardless of the obstacles placed on our path being conscious of the people around us can create an amazing outcome.

❋ What connections were created for you in Chapter 17?

Chapter 18

Love

"Cyrina, it is all about love," are the words I heard from Father Thomas Keating. I spoke about him earlier as someone who had a profound effect on me. I think about this statement often and feel so thankful that Father Keating shared this affirmation of love with me. We know we are energy beings and our emotion of love is on a higher frequency than jealousy. In our world today, many actions are driven by money, success, fancy things, jealousy, hate, and self-centeredness. So many people are still living by the old competitive state of keeping up with the Joneses. How can we possibly feel good in our hearts with some of these motivators? Yes, we recognize success as a positive motivator, although we must ask ourselves: "At what cost?"

We have all heard of those who are financially successful, even billionaires, yet they are not happy! Some have become "successful" through the drug cartels, stealing and killing their way into owning fancy and expensive things. But is this really what defines success? There are also the billionaires who are true to themselves, are philanthropists, and love their lives! Both sides of the spectrum are seen on every financial level.

These thoughts make me want to introduce you to an engrossing documentary: *I AM*. Tom Shadyac was the director of *I AM*, whose previous work includes *Ace Ventura, Patch Adams, The Nutty Professor*, and many other hilarious movies. In 2007, Tom Shadyac suffered a head injury, secondary to a bicycle accident that caused him to question his life and purpose. As a result, he was inspired to make this inspiring documentary titled *I AM*. In this movie, he interviews many people, ranging from scientists to philosophers. He shares their expertise and thoughts about our world. It is a thought-provoking documentary and I highly encourage you to invest some time to watch this movie.

In the movie, Tom Shadyac interviews his father, Richard Shadyac, who was a lawyer for St. Jude's Hospital. Richard Shadyac worked with Danny Thomas to create the Children's Research Hospital. Tom's brother, Richard C. Shadyac Jr., is now the CEO of a fundraising and awareness organization for St. Jude Children's Research Hospital. I had the incredible opportunity to meet Tom Shadyac at an event for St. Jude's Hospital. He was graciously kind and we talked about how we both experienced a similar situation with secondary head injuries due to bicycle accidents.

At this event, Shadyac shared the story about the inception of St. Jude Children's Research Hospital. When Danny Thomas's wife was pregnant with Marlo, he had been worried about financing the delivery of their child. He had prayed to St. Jude, asking for help. He promised to do something amazing in St. Jude's name if the resources arrived. Shortly after this prayer, he received a check in the mail that would cover the cost of her delivery. This was the sign he needed. After succeeding in his career and securing the necessary resources, he followed through and did something philanthropic in St. Jude's name.

"The mission of St. Jude Children's Research Hospital is to advance cures, and means of prevention, for catastrophic pediatric diseases through research and treatment. Consistent with the vision of our founder Danny Thomas, no child is denied treatment based on race, religion, or a family's ability to pay."

I am sharing this next story to illustrate how connected we all are in our world! My cousin Tom Aiello played a huge role in helping Drew, his nephew, receive treatment at St. Jude Children's Research Hospital. Drew was diagnosed with Acute Lymphoblastic Leukemia when he was just turning three years old. Tom at that time was the VP of PR with Sears and Sears holdings. Through his work there, they raised funds for St. Jude, plus, he knew Marlo Thomas professionally. He reached out to her and was able to help facilitate Drew becoming a patient at St. Jude and receiving the best treatment available.

Shawna Birdsall, Drew's mom, shared with me this touching story. *"One year prior to Drew being diagnosed, Tom had invited me and my husband, Dan, to a St. Jude fundraiser in Chicago. He had extra seats available through Sears, and he knew we would be in town and might enjoy the event. It was at this event we learned about St. Jude and its life-saving mission. That night, I said to my husband, "I cannot even imagine what these families have been through. What if it was Drew?" And a year later, it was Drew. Coincidence, fate, divine intervention...any way you look at it, we were meant to be at that event."*

During Drew's treatment, Drew's parents, Shawna and Dan, along with Drew's grandparents, Sue and Dave Birdsall, felt an overwhelming desire to join Danny Thomas' mission, *"No child should die in the dawn of life."* They began hosting an annual fundraiser called *Hope in the Hamptons* benefiting St. Jude Children's Research Hospital, and after five years, they have raised over two million dollars! Their extremely challenging situation gave birth to this remarkable fundraiser. St. Jude Hospital helped their son survive and thrive, and they are now able to help many other children have the chance to do the same. Thank you to the Birdsall family for the incredible gift of love you are giving to our world!

I had become closely acquainted with St. Jude's since Drew was a patient there. They shared with me how exceptional the staff and people had been at the hospital. Thankfully Drew, who is such an inspiring person, is thriving and living a normal and healthy life in remission after two and a half years of fantastic care at St. Jude. I have to add he is ready to ROAR in his life. Yes, he loves Katy Perry and this song. Here is to you, Drew!

Miraculous things can happen when we approach certain situations with love. No one person, institution, religion, business, or country has all the answers. We are all on the path of hopefully growing and evolving into the best person, company, or world we can be.

Now, how many of you know what GNH means? It is the acronym that stands for Gross National Happiness, first introduced by the country of Bhutan. King Wangchuck used the terminology 'GNH' during an interview in 1979. He said, *"We do not believe in Gross National Product. Gross National Happiness is more important."* In 2008 Bhutan was able to incorporate Gross National Happiness into its constitution. They say: *"The state shall strive to promote those conditions that will enable the pursuit of Gross National Happiness."*

The graph illustrates the nine domains of Gross National Happiness in Bhutan. A definition of 'domain' that resonates with me by the Cambridge Dictionary is: *"An area of interest or an area over which a person has control."* These are independent variables that can function together to bring more happiness. The list of the nine domains that are factored into their Gross National Happiness includes health, education, environment, community vitality, time use, psychological well-being, good governance, cultural resilience and promotion, and living standards.

While researching this subject for a talk that I presented in Toastmasters I learned about the culture and the values in Bhutan and found them fascinating! I was shocked to discover they did not introduce television or the internet to their country until 1999. They are also extremely conscientious about their carbon footprint. Therefore, any wrappers or trash brought into the country must be taken out.

It is interesting that 2/3 of their population, which is about 66% of people, get at least eight hours of sleep a night. This habit alone can bring much more happiness to our world. The impact of good sleep on improving our happiness, health, and productivity is well-documented. I find it very inspiring that the majority of a country's population gets a good night's rest. We all know that when we are tired, we are more likely to react and not respond mindfully. And when we react it can make conversations challenging to the point that they can escalate in a not-so-desirable direction.

June Silny wrote an article in Happify Daily entitled *"What's So Great About Happiness, Anyway? (The answer: plenty!)"*. In this piece, she listed 14 things that are improved by happiness. The listed outcomes have many layers to them. Specifically, her article focuses on the belief that happy people are more successful. Success is seen in many different domains. Happy people are more successful in relationships (friendship and marriage), career performance, income, health, and longevity. Happy people smile more often, are more helpful, exercise more, and eat healthier. They are also more productive and creative. These are only a few of the highlights from the article. I highly recommend that we all try this practice of happiness with its great side effects.

As soon as we wake up in the morning, we can allow ourselves to set the intention: *"I choose happiness,"* and set strategies to make this a reality. There are times in our lives when we have to hit the reset button. Sometimes we can be in a dark place but being conscious about our state and engineering a proactive shift is important. I want to encourage us all to live a day by design, not a day of default!

I read a great book, *The Happiness Project* by Gretchen Rubin, an amazing resource. Rubin conducted her *Happiness Project* over the course of a year. Each month, she introduced a new activity to focus on to bring more happiness into her life. As she mentioned in the book, we are all different and therefore different things bring us happiness. She says she is happier now than she was before she began "*The Happiness Project*" year.

We each have a brain and a mind. What is the difference between the two? The brain can be thought of as the hardware and the mind as the software. The Merriam-Webster Dictionary definition of 'mind' is: "*The element or complex of elements in an individual that feels, perceives, thinks, wills, and especially reasons.*" This is a very thought-provoking definition since we know that humans have a massive amount of thoughts per day.

In the HuffPost from May 23, 2013, an article titled "*There Are 50,000 Thoughts Standing between You and Your Partner Every Day!*" The author, Bruce Davis Ph.D. brings up great points about our thoughts and their effects on our relationships!

According to Dr. Davis:

"*When we have between 50,000-70,000 thoughts per day, this means between 35 and 48 thoughts per minute per person. The steady flow of thinking is a thick filter between our thoughts and feelings, our head and heart. The constant mental traffic prevents us from seeing clearly, listening deeply, and feeling our well of being.*"

His statement makes one think, *how can we be present if our minds are running like crazy?* You have to practice the intention to be present and mindful of our surroundings and the people around us!

With thousands of thoughts racing through our minds every day, there are those gremlins I talked about earlier that like to access our thoughts. These gremlins edit in the negative thoughts that limit us; these are the thoughts that cause us to say we cannot accomplish X, Y, or Z.

When I was young, I thought that I was the only one with these gremlins in my thoughts. It was after starting this journey of awareness that I realized the gremlins hijack everyone's minds at times. That said, I do believe that we need to stop limiting ourselves, and instead allow ourselves to shine bringing our best selves forward with confidence. I also know that this, unfortunately, is easier said than done.

In our world, we are faced with so many different distractions. People are continually looking at their phones and losing contact with the people right in front of them. I call the cell phone an electronic leash! I want to encourage you to allow yourself to go somewhere without your phone and see what occurs. It will help you be more present with whomever you are with and yourself.

When we are present with the people surrounding us, we may see a difference in the results we get. The filter that we see the world through shifts so that we have a more positive outlook. When we are faced with significant challenges in life, it is essential to allow ourselves to be and feel the way we do. Honesty about our feelings is crucial.

However, we can limit the amount of time that we allow ourselves to be in a funk or a sad state. That way, we can let ourselves shift from a negative state and move through the challenging times of our lives with grace. We can reframe and reconstruct our view of the situation we are facing and make decisions on how we can deal with each day as it comes. We do not want to allow ourselves to stay stagnant in this depleting mindset for a week, a month, a year, or years. We all know people who are still complaining about how they were mistreated in 1990. Let us all move on and not allow ourselves to be held back in any way from the past! With that said, for certain events in life we do require an extended duration to grieve and move through the pain.

Many times, in my life I have been challenged, not on a small scale, but a substantially high level of challenges. Now, more than ever, I do believe that these challenges were lessons, and ultimately provided me with a plethora of benefits. Many people say my approach to life is about making lemonade out of lemons. I am fortunate in my life that I have always seen the light through the darkness. I am not sure where this attitude came from, although I have always felt loved. I have amazing family and friends, which may have facilitated this outlook. Feeling loved has given me the strength and confidence to attack these challenges with optimism. This brings me back to what Thomas Keating said: *"Cyrina, it is all about love."*

We have a choice to stay in the dark or to allow a glimmer of light in by allowing some positivity to flow into our day. Where would you rather stay, in the dark or the light? Since this life is short, it is important to allow the light on your path. Now we are becoming more aware that thoughts are energy, and we know that energy creates mass; thank you, Einstein. Our thoughts bring much more to our world than we previously knew. There is a plethora of remarkable brain science that exists, although there is so much more to learn. Considering my double head trauma history, I am very interested in this research. We have a Reticular

Activating Systems (RAS) in our brains. Presently, I am learning more about the fascinating functions of the RAS and understanding the correlations researchers draw about its functions. The RAS is like a filter or the bouncer of your mind, that allows only certain things into the brain. Our brains could not handle all the constant stimuli, if it were not for this filter, there could be a potential overload, and we might short circuit. I find it interesting how our subconscious mind plays such a role in what we tell ourselves and the negative information that we allow in our thoughts.

With modern technology, it is amazing the amount of information we have available at our fingertips at any time! I am a junkie for TED Talks and YouTube videos! We are exposed to so many different people and ideas...what a gift!

We have to be open to the miraculous things occurring daily in our life. If we are not present and open, I feel we miss a lot of what has been purposely placed on our paths. *"The past is history, the future is a mystery, and the moment is a present."* There are many versions of this quote, similar ones shared by Elenor Roosevelt and Bil Keane. My heart tells me the more we are in the moment, the more presents that we will be able to see and attract.

Thankfully, I have not been scared to reach out to people, and I have allowed myself to listen to my intuition. If you do not reach out, you never know what potential outcome can occur. I reached out and sent that email to Mo Gawdat because I never know what will evolve from an action. As long as my actions are not hurting anyone, and my intentions are good, I should 'go for it!' What is the worst that can happen? You can allow yourself to know your desires and boundaries and then learn to listen and act on them.

Our life journey at times can look very different than the one we had initially envisioned. When I was younger, I always believed I would grow up, go to college, get married, buy a house, and have children, The American dream, right? My path did not unravel as originally planned. With that said, I am living an amazing life. I have many friends whom I have known since before they were married or had children. I am fortunate enough to feel close and connected with their children. Their children feel comfortable with me, or at least, I hope so. At this time in my life, that part of the equation, to biologically have children, has passed.

Honored and excited to have been able to fly my girlfriend Julie's daughter, Eloise, out to Colorado and to spend 10 days with her. Eloise, who was 15 at the time, is such an intelligent and beautiful (inside and outside) young lady. She has grown up in a very different world than the average person. At age 15, she had already lived in New York City, Sydney, Paris, and in Deland. She has a supermodel mom and a father who is a fashion photographer. Not your average life or experience by any means!

When Eloise arrived in Denver, I picked her up at the airport, and our adventure began. I was very cognizant of the fact that children of her age were, in general, completely attached to their phones. So, I did make one request for her to try and put her phone away since this was our time together. I did say if she had something that she needed to take care of, then, of course, use her phone. This was probably one of the best requests I have ever made in my life!

I wanted Eloise to meet my girlfriends, who have different careers. Exposing her to the various career paths one can follow and open her eyes to worlds other than her own. Excited to have so many friends who were able to meet, hang out, and answer questions, Eloise asked about them, their careers, and their paths.

Eloise and I also had time to spend alone in the mountains. We went to Breckenridge and Aspen where we rode bikes, hiked, and went out for nice dinners. We had such great conversations and enjoyed the beauty that surrounded us. My father inspired one conversation that we had. I shared with Eloise something my father had said to me when I was around her age: *"Do not be in a hurry to lose your innocence because once it is gone you cannot get it back."* I also shared with her: In life, you will often be tempted to do things that are not indicative of you and your beliefs, so please be true to what your heart says. If at that time in your life, your heart says, 'yes, this is what I should do' then listen, but if it says, 'no,' allow yourself to be strong and say no, and follow your heart.

If you listen to your heart at that time, you will not have to look back and say, *"I wish I had not done such-and-such activity."* If your actions have been in line with what your heart thought was right for you at that time, then regardless of the outcome, at least you had listened to your heart. This can rarely steer you wrong. I was impressed and surprised by Eloise's ability to be present in the moment and not looking at her phone! The only time she looked at her phone was at nighttime before we went to sleep.

Eloise and I built a stronger and more amazing connection during her visit. She wrote me a lovely letter expressing her love for me and her appreciation for our time together. I am so thankful to feel I have such incredible relationships with the young people in my life. While I am not sure what my role is supposed to be, hopefully, I am making a positive impact on the young people in my life.

Takeaway Lessons from this Chapter:

❋ Being in the moment can help us take note of the presents that surround us.

❋ Listen to your heart.

❋ We cannot control all that happens in our world, although we can control our reaction to the situations.

❋ Having young people in our lives can keep us up to date with new technology, music, and many other areas of interest.

❋ Connections with others and building relationships are the fuel to help keep happiness in our lives.

❋ Watch *I AM* by Tom Shadyac. In my eyes, it is an incredibly thought-provoking movie!

❋ The most conscious connection created in this chapter of my life was a connection with Eloise. I may not be a mother, but I can still have a positive impact on the children in my life.

❋ What connections were created for you in Chapter 18?

Chapter 19

Learning and Growth

My traumatic brain injury, compounded by a second head injury, inspired me to learn more about the brain. I wanted to use that knowledge to help optimize the health of my body and brain. I learned many things benefit the healing of the brain, yet they are not necessarily the traditional routes taken to treat head injuries.

The power of our minds, thoughts, and bodies, combined with the intriguing neuroplasticity of our brains makes for a relatively new area in the world of science. Yes, we know the physiology of the body is a huge factor in our health, but there is a new mindset that focuses on treating the whole person. This means: not just focusing on the body, but also on the mind, spirit, and energy that we create and that surrounds us. To optimize these areas and make sure they are all in sync with each other, in a state of harmony, can help facilitate our health to thrive.

I want to encourage actions that are in line with our moral compass and also noticing how our words and actions make our hearts feel. During the last 10 years, the medical world has learned a vast amount of information about the amazing healing modalities developed to help the brain. It is fascinating that many of these new healing modalities do not have any financial cost attached to them.

Whether they generate money or not, all resources should be shared, to help optimize someone's healing journey and their life. Money has been the impetus for wonderful creations, inventions, technological evolution, and a myriad of other great things. But there could be more organizations whose main goal is not financial gain, but research, to help people live their best lives!

The treatment modalities we are offered do not need to be all about the potential financial profitability. They can be stimulated by the desire to create healing and share new science to help the world. Craig Hospital, as I have already stated, has exceptional staff and resources. Being an alumnus, I was somewhat surprised I did not learn about many of these healing modalities during the extended time spent there as a patient. Things at Craig Hospital have shifted and changed in the years since. This is my personal experience, from many years ago.

I am mentioning this again since I am so intrigued by the fact that I had never heard of Brain-Derived Neurotrophic Factor before I read the book, *Spark: The Revolutionary New Science of Exercise and the Brain* by John J. Ratey and Eric Hagerman. It was fascinating to learn about the importance and role of BDNF produced in our brains. I realized that whether you have had an injury or not, exercise alone can help with cognition. Obviously, after a head injury, there needs to be a lot of downtime and clearance from one's doctor before returning to exercise. However, I am confident that being a very active person before my bike accident expedited my healing process.

Another extraordinarily insightful book I mentioned earlier that I read is, *The 5 Second Rule: Transform your Life, Work, and Confidence with Everyday Courage* by Mel Robbins. Mel is refreshingly open and shares her story of the struggles with anxiety and having to be medicated for many years. In her book, she talks about how '*The 5 Second Rule*' created a dramatic shift in her life. The life-changing gift that Mel has shared with our world has had a powerful impact on many lives. At the same time, it is important to acknowledge that we are all different. Some people absolutely need to be on medication, although this tool could be a positive complement to help with anxiety. Regardless, one needs to be honest with oneself, and seeking medical care is important if one is feeling like they need help.

There is science behind the simple tool that Mel Robbins shares in her book. This tool can help us to switch mental gears and gain more control over our thoughts and actions; in turn, this allows us to become empowered and our best. Unfortunately, so many of us have disempowering thoughts racing through our minds that we need to learn to control and edit. We also need to embrace more empowering ideas to allow ourselves to be our best cheerleaders. This aspect is particularly fascinating because we are now becoming citizens of a much more conscious world, where we allow ourselves to talk about our challenges. Let's face it; we all have them. Being more vulnerable and authentic helps our world to grow, heal, evolve and to have positive expansion. May our path be strewn with tools that can help us as we move through the hard times in life.

If we had a person in our lives who was as degrading and disempowering as our own gremlin thoughts, we would never be friends, much less spend any time with them. We must shift gears and stop the mental chatter of these disempowering words and thoughts, granting ourselves an empowering belief structure. We all have a different time frame, although it is never too late to gain the ability to be kind to ourselves and to evolve as empowered individuals.

This is a fact: we all have a purpose in this world! Remember the secret code I shared, P^3? We all have Purpose, Passion, and endless Possibilities. You are not an accident. You are meant to be here! I also want to encourage you to use the secret code, P^3, allowing attention to this truth and more energy to flow in this direction. As I shared earlier, there was only one in potentially 500 million chances that you would have been born. Your sperm won! These statistics affirm that you are here for a reason, you are not an accident and that you have a purpose!

We often have to be resilient to move through our challenging days. We have to keep telling ourselves that we have a purpose, and we are meant to be here. I had the fortunate opportunity to meet Dr. Edith Eva Eger, who is the author of *The Choice: Embrace the Possible*. She is a quintessential example of resilience. She kept moving forward, not letting her challenges defeat her spirit. She is an illustration of the strength that is inside of us. We need to nourish and believe in this strength. Dr. Eger is a holocaust survivor, and in her book, she shares some of the unbelievably awful experiences she endured! She also shared the beauty that blossomed after these extremely challenging days. She is such an inspiration and is a gift to our world! I am very thankful that she dared to share her story, one that has the power to inspire our world to be more resilient. Thank you, Edie, for the incredible gift you have shared!

We all have to find the strength to move through challenging days. That mind chatter I was speaking about earlier needs to have an outlet, and it needs to be released. Meditation, as I mentioned earlier, is another invaluable gift that the East has had its finger on the pulse of for thousands of years. While this astonishing tool does not cost anything, it does require time and intention. When making decisions in our lives, we have to measure the cost versus benefit of certain endeavors. Meditation, I feel, is well worth the time and energy spent!

This brings me back to HeartMath®, which is another incredible resource that shares with us the importance of the heart and the positive effects it can have on us and our physiology. Yes, there are initial fees to be trained in the practice. However, once you have learned these simple techniques, you can do them anywhere, and on the go. If you want to have sustained results, you have to be persistent with your practice, just like any other exercise. Once you have the practice down, you can make shifts quickly from a stressed state to a calm state.

There are so many potential nontraditional healing modalities that are effective. I am not acquainted with all of them, although I intend to allow myself to be open to continue to learn.

These are the things that I have learned and have come to believe along my journey:

* Love plays such a vital role in our life.

* I do not care how fancy your car or home is; I care about you and your character as a human being.

* We all have P³, Purpose, Passion and endless Possibilities;

* Meditation is a practice that can allow you to be more centered, focused, sleep better, and increase your productivity.

* Do not limit yourself. Allow yourself to be open to opportunities and keep your eyes open to see them.

* Laughter can help improve your health, day and life. I encourage you to share jokes. Here's one: "What bees make milk? Boo-Bees!" author unknown.

* Respect different opinions. You don't have to agree with others but have curiosity to understand why someone believes what they do and interact in a respectful way. This approach may lead to growth for both parties.

* Making plans, with follow-through to have fun, is important. If you don't, time just floats by without fun or a break from the grind.

* Out of tragedy, something wonderful can arise.

* I am amazed at how so many people are fake. I encourage you to be true to yourself, and you will find others who resonate with you and your truth. Grant yourself the gift of being YOU!

* We all have strengths and weaknesses. Allow yourself to let your strength shine and do not beat yourself up about your weakness.

* Worrying is a waste of time.

* Allow fear to motivate you to take action, not paralyze you!

* "Your behavior, attitude, and words can have a ripple effect. Choose them wisely."

<u>Amazing books</u>:

❀ *The Proof of Heaven* by Dr. Eben Alexander

❀ *The Telomere Effect: A Revolutionary Approach to Living Younger, Healthier, Longer* by Elizabeth Blackburn and Dr. Elissa Epel

❀ *The Choice Embrace the Possible* by Dr. Edith Eva Eger

❀ *Solve for Happy* by Mo Gawdat

❀ *Conversational Intelligence: How Great Leaders Build Trust and Get Extraordinary Results* by Judith E. Glaser

❀ *You Can Heal Your Life* by Louise Hay

❀ *Think and Grow Rich* by Napoleon Hill

❀ *Code of the Extraordinary Mind: 10 Unconventional Laws to Redefine Your Life and Succeed on Your Own Terms* by Vishen Lakhiani

❀ *The Power of Eight: Harnessing the Miraculous Energies of a Small Group to Heal Others, Your Life, and the World* by Lynn McTaggart

❀ *Dying to be Me* by Anita Moorjani

❀ *The Energy Codes: The 7-Step System to Awaken Your Spirit, Heal Your Body, and Live Your Best Life* by Dr. Sue Morter

❀ *UnDo It!: How Simple Lifestyle Changes Can Reverse Most Chronic Diseases* by Anne Ornish and Dean Ornish

❀ *Spark: The Revolutionary New Science of Exercise and the Brain* by John J. Ratey & Eric Hagerman

❀ *The 5 Second Rule: Transform your Life, Work, and Confidence with Everyday Courage* by Mel Robbins.

❀ *You are a Badass* by Jen Sincero

❀ *Autobiography of a Yogi* by Paramhansa Yogananda

❀ *The Seat of the Soul* by Gary Zukav

In my mind, these are all phenomenal and thought-provoking books that will allow you to expand.

Influential Teachers:

After my bike accident, I was exposed to so many amazing teachers. Most of these teachers I have never met, although I have studied what they teach, or taught. I want to share many of them with you and encourage you to explore this list. I hope that one may resonate with you and facilitate your expansion as they have mine.

* Shawn Achor
* John Assaraf
* Dr. Elizabeth H. Blackburn
* Gregg Braden
* Brendon Burchard
* Les Brown
* Jim Bunch
* Jack Canfield
* Dr. Deepak Chopra
* Dr. Joe Dispenza
* Mike Dooley
* Dr. Wayne Dyer
* Mo Gawdat
* Judith E. Glaser
* Dean Graziosi
* David R. Hamilton
* Louise Hay
* Napoleon Hill
* Father Thomas Keating
* Jenna Kutcher
* Vishen Lakhiani

* Dr. Bruce Lipton

* Dr. Sonja Lyubomirsky

* Lynn McTaggart

* Kane and Alessia Minkus

* Mary Morrissey

* Dr. Sue Morter

* Dr. Christiane Northrup

* Gina Pigott

* Mel Robbins

* Tony Robbins

* Dr. Mona Lisa Schultz. I had a fantastic summer camp in Maine with Dr. Schultz that started on 7/7/14. Interesting date, isn't it? 7 +7 = 14. It was an unforgettable experience.

* Oprah Winfrey

* KellyAnne Zielinski

Takeaway Lessons from this Chapter:

* Exercise is vital and has a powerful irrefutable impact on the body and brain.

* Meditation has many potentially substantial positive effects on our life.

* Our thoughts and actions have an immense impact on our lives and connections; choose wisely.

* There are many amazing teachers in our world! Find some that resonate with you. It is crucial to expand and allow oneself to learn, evolve, and grow.

* We are all energy beings. The important questions to answer are: What energy are we surrounded by? And what energy are we feeding the field?

* The most conscious connection created in this chapter of my life was a connection with the influential teachers in my life. I feel so

grateful for all the guidance that has been shared by the amazing teachers that guide me along my journey.

❋ What connections were created for you in Chapter 19?

Chapter 20

Expansion

We know life can present us with hurdles and can seem very dark at times. However, there is always a glimmer of light, and we must encourage ourselves to see that light. I will again share some of the tools that have helped me on this journey. This is a reminder for when we need to fill our toolbox with tools to help us move past the challenges we face. Will our focus go toward the darkness or the light? This decision can have a significant impact on our lives.

By being present in the moment, we will be more apt to see all the magical things that surround us. The amazing gifts in our world can inspire us to be the best that we can be. I'm hoping my story has illustrated the challenging times I faced in my life, along with the invaluable experiences and support I received. I am thankful that I never gave in to despair by feeling sorry for myself, and that I was able to move to the beautiful side of the obstacles.

With that said, I have to confess that there have been days when I needed to cry and let out the built-up frustration. Releasing the anger, stress, or whatever depleting emotion one may be experiencing is key. I share this because letting all those emotions out decreases the feelings of being overwhelmed; in turn, this helps us move through life a bit more easily. It gives us the ability to hit the reset button and not to let those emotions hold us back. Yes, we all have our depleting feelings and thoughts, but let's not give them control over us.

There are many tools that we can put in our toolbox to help us on this journey. I encourage everyone to explore and see what the best methods are for you. I feel blessed that I have been introduced to many different modalities that have helped me to maintain my optimism, resilience and my strength when things have become challenging. In the times when it feels impossible to move to the other side of the obstacle, we can open our toolbox. Finding the right tool that can help us to keep moving forward and emerge successfully on the other side. Creating your toolbox will be time well spent! We are all different, so explore and find the methods that work best to help you move forward with an optimal mindset.

In this last chapter, I will be recapping the information shared earlier. My goal is to review the methods that I have witnessed making a positive impact. I use several daily tools in my life that have been helpful. The first tool is my daily RPM, a.k.a., 'Rest, Pee, Meditate.' I meditate for the first 20 minutes and 20 seconds of my day; it allows me to be calmer, more present and centered. Yes, I love the extrapolation of seeing 20/20 with my morning meditation! While meditating, I am not always good at staying present, centered, and focused the entire time. Even so, I feel very confident that my life is calmer and happier than it would be without the practice of meditation. Being more present allows me to live with as little fear as possible of what my future holds.

When I lost my ability to be a pharmacist, I felt a lot of fear because I still have to support myself financially. Hopefully, the headaches and memory issues will leave me soon. I have had to develop the necessary trust that all will be okay in my life. Thankfully, I believe in a higher power who I call God, and I have the sense that these circumstances are part of a bigger plan! If I can keep my eyes open for the opportunities placed on my path, positive things will unfold.

HeartMath® is another useful and reliable tool that has helped me bring my best self forward. It has aided me to allow myself to feel calmer and be resilient regardless of the challenges in my day. At those times when I am feeling a sense of increased agitation or frustration, I use a HeartMath® tool. Their techniques facilitate calmness and allow a shift in my emotions while improving my ability to respond, not react. I can feel when my buttons are being pushed, and these tools allow me to feel more composure before I react with an action or statement I will regret.

Gratitude is another daily practice of mine. We now know, through science, that gratitude journaling helps to create more happiness in one's life. As I said earlier, you can place things on your list as small and simple as being thankful for a good cup of coffee, a good conversation, a smile, or a hug. This will help fill your gratitude journal and your heart, and it is an easy tool to implement in your life.

There is a lot of good and bad out in our world. When we set our intention, where will we allow our focus to go? Will we look for the positive in our lives or dwell on the negatives? It is our choice. When making this choice, let's remember the popular statement: *"Where your attention goes, energy flows."*

Smiling is another daily activity that I embrace and incorporate in my day. When we smile, we start to create chemicals in our bodies that will facilitate more happiness. We know that smiles are contagious; let's create a smiling virus.

Look up a joke and share some laughs. This can be a great daily activity. It is easy to Google jokes for the day, they even have apps for jokes! We can bring a little laughter to our day and make that fun connection with others. It could be an ingredient for some happiness in our day.

Feeling connected is one of my favorite daily activities that leads to more happiness. Making a conscious effort to connect with another person is a huge gift to me! I am passionate about people and want to know and understand who they are and what they believe. This is a driver in my life. The ability to share meaningful, authentic and vulnerable conversations is a skill set that I can bring to the table. I have found and continue to find the most interesting people through these interactions. We never know where these connections will lead!

Exercise is another frequent activity in my life. Although I may not work out daily, I try to work out at least five times a week. We know exercise helps produce the chemicals in our body that facilitate more happiness, brain health, and decreases anxiety and depression. As I mentioned earlier, I highly recommend John J. Ratey and Eric Hagerman's book, *Spark: The Revolutionary New Science of Exercise and the Brain.* This book shares the science behind some of the benefits that you receive from exercise. Hopefully, if appropriate, it will inspire you to incorporate more exercise into your life.

As we age, time seems to fly by so quickly that the days seem to roll right into each other. Being in the moment helps us to enjoy this journey called life and brings presents to our day. I encourage all of us to live a life that resonates with our hearts. If it does not resonate, there will potentially be some physiological effects that keep us from living our optimal life. This life is a gift to enjoy, so be happy along the way. We all have different challenges that confront us. We know that we cannot control all the challenges that are placed in our path, but we can control how we respond to the situation at hand.

With every challenge that I have faced, there have been several huge lessons learned, and many secondary wonderful gifts revealed. When we are faced with difficult times, we have to try to stay empowered. Knowing that we will get to the other side of this not-so-pleasant experience and having this mindset will help us to facilitate a better outcome.

When we become our worst critic, we often live up to our expectations and self-talk. The outcomes that we see are not that favorable. Quantum physics can enlighten us. I am not a physicist, but it does run in the family. My uncle is a physicist and has been a great source of information and perspective for me. Learning more about quantum mechanics has been a very eye-opening experience!

Eugene Wigner, a theoretical physicist, and mathematician said, *"It was not possible to formulate the laws of quantum mechanics in a fully consistent way without reference to consciousness."* This is a thought-provoking statement since the Cambridge Dictionary defines consciousness as *"The state of being awake, aware of what is around you, and able to think."* Remember: *"Everything is energy and that's all there is to it. Match the frequency of the reality you want, and you cannot help but get that reality. It can be no other way. This is not philosophy. This is physics."* May this quote encourage and inspire us to elevate our frequency to match our desired reality!

Life becomes so hectic and busy at times that we forget to live and enjoy this gift. If we can remain in the present moment, be kind and respectful to ourselves, and share that way of being with others, we can create an amazing ripple effect. This positive ripple can help the world catch and spread more happiness.

Sonja Lyubomirsky, Ph.D., a professor of psychology and a bestselling author, has shared some fascinating data about happiness that tells us we have a choice! The findings from her research offer layers of meaning, hope, and insight. She has found that our DNA determines only 50% of our happiness. Our DNA is passed down from our mom and dad. Yes, we cannot choose our DNA, but it is also a fact that our DNA is not our destiny. Her findings show that only 10% of our happiness is determined by our outside circumstances, such as our financial status, relationships, and living situation, which is quite eye-opening. Yes, some of us may be genetically predisposed to be happier, although 40% of what determines our happiness is our intentional activities, our thoughts, and actions. This data tells us that there is a lot of room for us to impact our happiness level. This is a chart to illustrate Dr. Lyubomirsky's data:

The 3 Determinants of Happiness

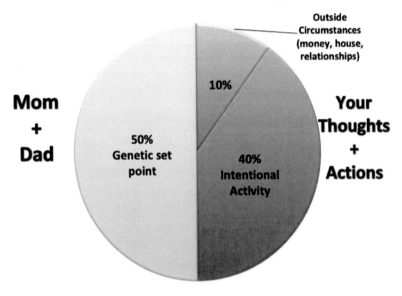

Outside Circumstances (money, house, relationships)

Mom + Dad

10%

50% Genetic set point

40% Intentional Activity

Your Thoughts + Actions

For this reason, I believe it is worth our time and energy to determine the thoughts and activities that bring us happiness. How do we want to live, by default or by design? May we allow a proactive intention to invite more ideas about the thoughts and activities that will foster more happiness in our lives! This activity will have a huge return on our investment! May we also be motivated to implement our findings of the thoughts and actions that bring happiness into our lives. Let us all optimize the 40% determination of our happiness that Dr. Lyubomirsky has shared with us to invite more happiness into our lives.

Here is an idea that I have developed, although not a scientifically proven idea, I've received great feedback from my clients and friends who have implemented this practice. The idea could help introduce more fun into our lives! This is a simple group activity. Each person is to write down on separate pieces of paper three group activities that bring them happiness; these activities should take around an hour, or whatever time frame you wish to experience. Then place all of the ideas in a jar. Once a week, or whenever you are together, draw from the jar and everyone can participate in the chosen activity. You may want to pull out the idea the night before to ensure you have all the necessary ingredients or equipment.

If during the activity, we allow ourselves to put away our phones, turn off the TV and become more present, it helps us to develop a stronger connection. If you're playing with your family, let everyone be silly. Parents, you can nourish your inner child for this short period. Some ideas for activities are dancing, singing, card games, board games, hiking, riding bikes or cooking together. If you have children, you can even make *"Mocktails."* They are non-alcoholic and flavorful drinks. We can be creative and invite happiness to our day by bringing more adventures and fun to our lives!

This life is a gift! The fact that I have almost died three times in my life makes me very aware of this truth. My life-changing experiences became the impetus for sharing my story, with the desire to spread more happiness. Every day, may we all enjoy elements of our life, be present, say good-bye to fear and hello to love, raise our frequency, and help the world Catch Happiness®!

Takeaway Lessons from this Chapter:

❉ We have choices!

❉ We can create a positive ripple effect.

❉ Our thoughts and actions not only affect us, but they also affect the world. Being conscious of this can help us choose our thoughts and actions wisely.

❉ Enjoying our day and the lovely moments helps to create more beauty in our lives.

❉ Every relationship, (friendship, romantic, professional or acquaintance), whether it lasts for a day, a week, a year, or a lifetime comes with its lessons and growth, which can be hard to see at times.

❉ The science of quantum physics is opening our world by showing us that we can have an impact on the outcome of our lives. Let us all make a quantum leap!

❉ According to Dr. Sonja Lyubomirsky's research, if we are proactive and invite more happy thoughts and actions into our life, we can help ourselves Catch Happiness®!

❉ May we all enjoy each day, be present, say good-bye to fear and hello to love and help the world Catch Happiness!

✳ The most conscious connection created in this chapter of my life was a connection with the knowledge that 40% of our happiness is determined by our thoughts and actions. I love the science behind happiness. So, let's fill our toolboxes to help the world Catch Happiness!

✳ What connections were created for you in Chapter 20?

References

Audio Books:

Achor, Shawn. *The Happiness Advantage: The Seven Principles of Positive Psychology That Fuel Success and Performance at Work*. Narrated by Shawn Achor. Random House Audio 2010. Audible.com, www.audible.com/pd/The-Happiness-Advantage-Audiobook/B0041NZRDC?pf_rd_p=e81b7c27-6880-467a-b5a7-13cef5d729fe&pf_rd_r=DG3X61X2J2GKNXJ8DKM6&qid=1580768944&ref=a_search_c3_1Product_1_1&sr=1-1.

Alexander, Eben. *The Proof of Heaven*. Narrated by Eben Alexander, Hachette Audio 2012. Audible.com, www.audible.com/pd/Proof-of-Heaven-Audiobook/B009HTF9TM.

Blackburn, Elizabeth, Epel, Elissa. *The Telomere Effect: A Revolutionary Approach to Living Younger, Healthier, Longer*. Narrated by Suzanne Toren, Hatchette Audio 2017. Audible.com, www.audible.com/pd/The-Telomere-Effect-Audiobook/B01N43RX2R?qid=1580769454&sr=1-1&pf_rd_p=e81b7c27-6880-467a-b5a7-13cef5d729fe&pf_rd_r=DY6D4S0MXMDY9S4R2P7H&ref=a_search_c3_1Product_1_1.

Brown, Brené. *Rising Strong*. Narrated by Brené Brown, Random House Audio 2015. Audible.com, www.audible.com/pd/Rising-Strong-Audiobook/B00VSEM9QK?qid=1580770276&sr=1-1&pf_rd_p=e81b7c27-6880-467a-b5a7-13cef5d729fe&pf_rd_r=DJGMZF27Q6X5YWYG2CS2&ref=a_search_c3_1Product_1_1.

Byrne, Rhonda. *The Secret*. Narrated by Rhonda Byrne, Simon & Schuster Audio 2006. Audible.com, www.audible.com/pd/The-Secret-Audiobook/B002V5GN4Y?qid=1580780791&sr=1-1&pf_rd_p=e81b7c27-6880-467a-b5a7-

13cef5d729fe&pf_rd_r=BF7TENXD5VWKB5QAE1BG&ref=a_search_c3_lPr oduct_1_1.

Dispenza, Joe. *Becoming Supernatural: How Common People Are Doing the Uncommon*. Authors Republic 2018. Audiobooks.com, www.audiobooks.com/audiobook/becoming-supernatural-how-common-people-are-doing-the-uncommon/342505?refId=38712&gclid=Cj0KCQiApt_xBRDxARIsAAMUMu _SoGRe61Hoq5prdQqakO5eGHylbA__71O32fDjotI_TRYtFbMmBrUaArXfE ALw_wcB.

Eger, Eva, Edith. *The Choice: Embrace the Possible*. Narrated by Tovah Feldshuh, Simon & Schuster Audio 2017. Audible.com,

http://www.audible.com/search?keywords=the+choice+edith+eger&ref=.

Gawdat, Mo. *Solve for Happy: Engineer Your Path to Joy*. Narrated by Mo Gawdat, Simon & Schuster Audio 2017. Audible.com, www.audible.com/pd/Solve-for-Happy-Audiobook/B01N5R6LVS?qid=1580771129&sr=1-1&pf_rd_p=e81b7c27-6880-467a-b5a7-13cef5d729fe&pf_rd_r=84GX5NPH40YRBNPXX1TQ&ref=a_search_c3_lPro duct_1_1.

Glaser, Judith E. *Conversational Intelligence: How Great Leaders Build Trust and Get Extraordinary Results*. Narrated by Karen Saltus, Bibliomotion, Inc 2014. Audible.com, www.audible.com/pd/Conversational-Intelligence-Audiobook/B00I08AW1G?qid=1580771746&sr=1-1&pf_rd_p=e81b7c27-6880-467a-b5a7-13cef5d729fe&pf_rd_r=50QEP2M8W6T2EGPE34S0&ref=a_search_c3_lProdu ct_1_1.

Hamilton, David R. *The Five Side Effects of Kindness: This Book Will Make You Feel Better, Be Happier & Live Longer*. Narrated by David R Hamilton, Hay House 2017. Audible.com, www.audible.com/pd/The-Five-Side-Effects-of-Kindness-Audiobook/B06W2K482K?qid=1580771910&sr=1-1&pf_rd_p=e81b7c27-6880-467a-b5a7-

13cef5d729fe&pf_rd_r=NNDKTF3HFT9V6GY7ZYSP&ref=a_search_c3_lPro
duct_1_1.

Hill, Napoleon. *Outwitting the Devil: The Secret to Freedom and Success.*
Narrated by Dan John Miller, Phil Gigante, Brilliance Audio, 2011.
Audible.com, www.audible.com/pd/Napoleon-Hills-Outwitting-the-Devil-
Audiobook/B0051QF7L0?qid=1580780528&sr=1-1&pf_rd_p=e81b7c27-6880-
467a-b5a7-
13cef5d729fe&pf_rd_r=PZRG59VR52AAQWG29494&ref=a_search_c3_lProd
uct_1_1.

Hill, Napoleon. *Think and Grow Rich.* Narrated by Erik Synnestvedt, Gildan
Media, LLC 2017. Audible.com, www.audible.com/pd/Think-and-Grow-Rich-
Audiobook/B002V5D950?qid=1580772044&sr=1-1&pf_rd_p=e81b7c27-6880-
467a-b5a7-
13cef5d729fe&pf_rd_r=XCQ06D4A7M62SVHG1ERF&ref=a_search_c3_lProd
uct_1_1.

Lakhiani, Vishen. *Code of the Extraordinary Mind: 10 Unconventional Laws to
Redefine Your Life & Succeed on Your Own Terms.* Narrated by Vishen
Lakhiani, Simon & Schuster Audio 2016. Audible.com,
www.audible.com/pd/Think-and-Grow-Rich-
Audiobook/B002V5D950?qid=1580772044&sr=1-1&pf_rd_p=e81b7c27-6880-
467a-b5a7-
13cef5d729fe&pf_rd_r=XCQ06D4A7M62SVHG1ERF&ref=a_search_c3_lProd
uct_1_1.

Lipton, Bruce H. *The Biology of Belief.* Narrated by Dr. Bruce Lipton, Sounds
True 2006. Audible.com, www.audible.com/pd/The-Biology-of-Belief-
Audiobook/B002V013NU?qid=1580833800&sr=1-1&pf_rd_p=e81b7c27-6880-
467a-b5a7-
13cef5d729fe&pf_rd_r=8ADKJTTAC9YD6XX7846P&ref=a_search_c3_lProd
uct_1_1

Lyubomirsky, Sonja. *The Myths of Happiness: What Should Make You Happy,
but Doesn't, What Shouldn't Make You Happy, but Does.* Narrated by Kathy
Keane, Penguin Audio 2013. Audible.com, www.audible.com/pd/The-Myths-of-
Happiness-Audiobook/B00AWEDMRM?qid=1580772422&sr=1-

1&pf_rd_p=e81b7c27-6880-467a-b5a7-
13cef5d729fe&pf_rd_r=FKS79ZQYSYMQ09ZHEKAP&ref=a_search_c3_1Pro
duct_1_1.

Lyubomirsky, Sonja. *The How of Happiness: A Scientific Approach to Getting
the Life You Want.* Narrated by Dr. Sonja Lyubomirsky, Penguin Audio 2009.
Audible.com, www.audible.com/pd/The-How-of-Happiness-
Audiobook/B002V8DG0U?qid=1580772586&sr=1-2&pf_rd_p=e81b7c27-
6880-467a-b5a7-
13cef5d729fe&pf_rd_r=GES288RAEDQP5C0W5HQZ&ref=a_search_c3_1Pro
duct_1_2.

McTaggart, Lynn. *The Power of Eight: Harnessing the Miraculous Energies of
a Small Group to Heal Others, Your Life, and the World.* Narrated by Gabra
Zackman, Simon & Schuster Audio 2017. Scribd.com,
https://www.scribd.com/listen/359921738

Morter, Sue. *The Energy Codes: The 7-Step System to Awaken Your Spirit, Heal
Your Body, and Live Your Best Life.* Narrated by Dr. Sue Morter, Simon &
Schuster Audio 2019. Scribd.com, https://www.scribd.com/listen/390805925

Ornish, Dean, Ornish, Anne. *Undo It!: How Simple Lifestyle Changes Can
Reverse Most Chronic Diseases.* Narrated by Dean Ornish, Anne Ornish,
Random House Audio 2019. Audible.com, www.audible.com/pd/Undo-It-
Audiobook/B07L39P44F?qid=1580772996&sr=1-1&pf_rd_p=e81b7c27-6880-
467a-b5a7-
13cef5d729fe&pf_rd_r=TJMKD3EWKH9JY91CM16A&ref=a_search_c3_1Pro
duct_1_1.

Robbins, Mel. *The 5 Second Rule: Transform your Life, Work, and Confidence
with Everyday Courage.* Narrated by Mel Robbins, Mel Robbins Productions
Inc. 2017. Audible.com, www.audible.com/pd/The-5-Second-Rule-
Audiobook/B06VX22V89?qid=1580773256&sr=1-1&pf_rd_p=e81b7c27-6880-
467a-b5a7-
13cef5d729fe&pf_rd_r=A4MXJQEM9K4Y9TA1M3XJ&ref=a_search_c3_1Pro
duct_1_1.

Rosenthal, Norman E. *SUPER MIND – How to Boost Performance and Live a Richer and Happier Life through Transcendental Meditation.* Narrated by Dan Woren, Blackstone Audiobooks 2016. Audible.com, www.audible.com/search?searchAuthor=Norman+E.+Rosenthal+MD&pf_rd_p=e81b7c27-6880-467a-b5a7-13cef5d729fe&pf_rd_r=8FRX46GZWQ6969D6FTZY&ref=a_search_c3_lAuthor_1_1_1.

Rubin, Gretchen. *The Happiness Project: Or, Why I Spent a Year Trying to Sing in the Morning, Clean My Closets, Fight Right, Read Aristotle, and Generally Have More Fun.* Narrated by Gretchen Rubin, Harper Audio 2009. Audible.com, www.audible.com/pd/The-Happiness-Project-Audiobook/B0030MV7MU?qid=1580773747&sr=1-1&pf_rd_p=e81b7c27-6880-467a-b5a7-13cef5d729fe&pf_rd_r=10GKFAYFEQ84Q405NVNB&ref=a_search_c3_lProduct_1_1.

Sincero, Jen. *You Are a Badass: How to Stop Doubting Your Greatness and Start Living an Awesome Life.* Narrated by Jen Sincero, Tantor Audio 2013. Audible.com, www.audible.com/pd/You-Are-a-Badass-Audiobook/B00EYNQSGO?qid=1580773885&sr=1-1&pf_rd_p=e81b7c27-6880-467a-b5a7-13cef5d729fe&pf_rd_r=15GGWZMKGTMMXWBPBXYX&ref=a_search_c3_lProduct_1_1.

Yogananda, Paramhansa. *Autobiography of a Yogi.* Narrated by Swami Kriyananda, Crystal Clarity Publishers 2008. Audibe.com, www.audible.com/pd/Autobiography-of-a-Yogi-Audiobook/B002V1BJ1A?qid=1580774046&sr=1-2&pf_rd_p=e81b7c27-6880-467a-b5a7-13cef5d729fe&pf_rd_r=D6JA3AKJDABQF6NAW079&ref=a_search_c3_lProduct_1_2.

Zukav, Gary. *The Seat of the Soul: 25th Anniversary Edition.* Narrated by Gary Zukav, Maya Angelou, Oprah Winfrey, Simon and Schuster Audio 2014. Audible.com, www.audible.com/pd/The-Seat-of-the-Soul-

Audiobook/B002V5IXB0?qid=1580783092&sr=1-1&pf_rd_p=e81b7c27-6880-467a-b5a7-13cef5d729fe&pf_rd_r=G54N1NB858GRDGBX4AXK&ref=a_search_c3_lProduct_1_1.

Books:

Childre, Doc, et al. *Heart Intelligence: Connecting with Intuitive Guidance of the Heart*. Waterfront Press, 2016.

Childre, Doc, et al. *The HeartMath Solution.* HarperCollins, 2000.

Hay, Louise L.. *You Can Heal Your Life.* Hay House, Inc. 1984.

HeartMath® Institute. *The Inside Story: Understanding the Power of Feeling the Heart-Brain Connection*. HeartMath® Institute, 2002.

Ratey, John J. and Eric Hagerman. *Spark: The Revolutionary New Science of Exercise and the Brain.* Little, Brown and Company, 2008.

Liniger, Dave and Laura Morton. *My Next Step: An Extraordinary Journey of Healing and Hope*. Hay House, Inc. 2013.

Blog Post:

Dultz, Travis. Who said, "Yesterday is history tomorrow is a mystery today is a gift"? *Yesterday Tomorrow Today Phrase Origin*, 27 August 2015, www.yesterdaytomorrowtodaypresent.blogspot.com/, August 2015.

Articles from the Internet:

WhatIsEpigenetics. A Super Brief and Basic Explanation of Epigenetics for Total Beginners. www.whatisepigenetics.com/what-is-epigenetics/, 30 July 2018.

Davis, Bruce. "There Are 50,000 Thoughts Standing Between you and Your Partner Every Day!" *Huffpost*, www.huffpost.com/entry/healthy-relationships_b_3307916, 23 May 2013.

Silny, June. What's So Great About Happiness, Anyway? (The Answer: Plenty!). *Happify Daily*, www.happify.com/hd/whats-so-great-about-happiness/

Fernandez, Elizabeth. Lifestyle Changes May Lengthen Telomeres, A Measure of Cell Aging

Diet, Meditation, Exercise Can Improve Key Element of Immune Cell Aging, UCSF Scientists Report. *University of California San Francisco,*

www.ucsf.edu/news/2013/09/108886/lifestyle-changes-may-lengthen-telomeres-measure-cell-aging, 16 September 2013.

Stambor, Zak. (2006) A key to happiness Studies hint at possible ways to get off the hedonic treadmill and find lasting happiness. *American Psychological Association,* Vol 37, No 9 October 2006, page 34. www.apa.org/monitor/oct06/key, October 2006.

Event Speaker:

Mandossian, Alex. World Class Speaker 3 Day Conference. Kane and Alessia Minkus. San Francisco, June 2019.

Achor, Shawn. (2011, May). The happy secret to better work. TEDxBloomington. Talk presented at the 2011 TEDx conference, Bloomington, Indiana, U.S.A.

Movies:

Handy, Dagan. (Producer), & Shadyac, Tom. (Director). (2001). I Am. [Motion picture]. United Stated: Shady Acres Entertainment.

Heineman, Matthew, Froemke, Susan. (Producer), & Heineman, Matthew, Froemke, Susan. (Director). (2012). Escape Fire: The Fight to Rescue American Healthcare. [Motion Picture] United States: Roadside Attractions, Lionsgate.

Schiff, Paul, et al. & Lee, Jieho (Director). (2007). The Air I Breathe. [Motion picture]. United States: THINKFilm.

Websites:

HeartMath®. Studies conducted with over 11.500* people have shown improvements in mental & emotional well-being in just 6-9 weeks using *HeartMath* training and technology. www.heartmath.com/.

A Page on a Website or on the Internet:

Gregory, Alex. AlexGregory/Cartoonist/Googlesearch

Oursler, Fulton. www.brainyquote.com/quotes/fulton_oursler_175108

OPHI: Oxford Poverty & Human Development Initiative. Bhutan's Gross National Happiness Index. ophi.org.uk/policy/national-policy/gross-national-happiness-index/

Oursler, Fulton. Brainyquotes.com. www.brainyquote.com/quotes/fulton_oursler_175108

Rohn, Jim. https://www.goodreads.com/quotes/1798-you-are-the-average-of-the-five-people-you-spend

Shadyac, Richard C. Jr. www.stjude.org/directory/s/richard-c-shadyac.html

St. Jude's Mission. www.stjude.org/about-st-jude.html

Waddington, C. H. Wikipediapage.en.wikipedia.org/wiki/C._H._Waddington

Author

Dr. Cyrina Bullard has been a pharmacist for over 25 years and is now having to reinvent herself. She was guided to create <u>Catch Happiness</u>®. Instead of witnessing people catching and spreading infections, she has chosen to use science-based tools to encourage people to catch and spread more happiness! While Cyrina has almost died three times in her life, she has gained a great deal of wisdom through her journey.

She is certified by UC Berkeley in The Science of Happiness and by Yale in the Science of Well Being. She is certified in Conversational Intelligence® and is a Life Mastery Consultant through Mary Morrissey, LifeSOULutions That Work LLC. She is also a HeartMath® Certified Trainer and volunteers to teach resiliency training to the residents at Sacred Heart, a homeless shelter in Denver. Currently, she is on the Continuing Education Committee at the College of Pharmacy at the University of Colorado and the RMRBIS Consumer Advisory Board at Craig Hospital.

In her keynote speeches and workshops, she guides her audience to recognize how each individual has a purpose. Moreover, she shares the tools for resiliency, Conversational Intelligence®, as well as keys to creating daily happiness. Inspired to help people embrace and love the path they are traveling she looks forward to sharing scientifically-backed tools to help facilitate more happiness in our world.

Photo of Author by Garrett Hacking | PhotographyG.com

PostScript

       I am not a statistician, although I do believe, statistically speaking, it would be more likely that I would win the lottery than what I am about to share with you to occur. This experience without a doubt is a beacon to grant me the serenity that I am on the right path! In May of 2019, I tried to get the domain name <u>CreatingConsciousConnecections.com</u> for my book, and it was not available.

       September of 2019, I was on the phone with a friend, we had not spoken in quite a long while. Sharing the title of my book with her, she asked me to repeat the title and then said, I feel like we are surrounded by angels right now. Curious, I said, why do you say that? She said, "Literally just three days prior I rebranded my website to <u>Sarabfit.com</u> and previously it was <u>CreatingConsciousConnections.com</u>." How is this even possible?? She gifted me with the domain name! Sara, thank you so much for your generosity! It will be exciting to see where this magic will lead!